TECHNICAL ANALYSIS FOR TRADING INDEX WARRANTS

Strategies and Index-Linked Investments to Build and Protect a Share Portfolio

CHRIS TEMBY

Wrightbooks

ACKNOWLEDGMENTS

Most index charts produced by SuperCharts 4 using data supplied by Almax. 97 year charts provided by Colin Nicholson. Stock charts supplied by Phillips Henderson Ward using AAP data. Advance/Decline line charts produced by Ezy Charts with data supplied by Electronic Information Solutions. The All Ordinaries Accumulation/Price Indices figure in Chapter 2 is reproduced from the *ASX Journal* with the permission of the Australian Stock Exchange Limited.

I would like to thank those who have assisted in various ways in making this book possible: Owen Davis for ideas and editing, David Robinson of Phillips Henderson Ward Limited stock brokers for answers to myriad questions, Colin Nicholson of the Australian Technical Analysts Association for editing and constructive comments, the ATAA for providing a forum for learning and discussion, Jody Elliss of Electronic Information Solutions for supplying Ezy Chart software and historic data, Russell Lander of Dicksons stock brokers for data on the Value Line Index, Jonathon Kur of Hogan & Partners stock brokers for information on short selling, and my dear wife Heather for TLC during the long months of writing.

Wrightbooks Pty Ltd   PO Box 270   Elsternwick   Victoria   3185
Ph: (03) 9532 7082   Fax: (03) 9532 7084   Email: wbooks@ozemail.com.au
Web Site www.wrightbooks.com.au

National Library of Australia Cataloguing-in-publication data:

Temby, Chris.

Technical analysis for trading index warrants: strategies and index-linked investments to build and protect a share portfolio.

Bibliography.

Includes index.

ISBN 1 875857 75 3.

1. Stock options - Australia. 2. Stock warrants - Australia. 3. Investments - Australia. 4. Portfolio management - Australia. I. Title.

332.63220994

Cover design by Rob Cowpe
Printed in Australia by Griffin Press

ISBN: 1 875857 75 3

DISCLAIMER

Contents

Contents (cont'd)

Dedication

To all those investors who just want their nest-egg to grow satisfactorily each year, but without having to spend many hours each week on monitoring, analysis and information overload

Part I

SETTING THE STAGE

Chapter 1

INTRODUCTION

IT HAS LONG BEEN recognised that buying quality equities at the start of bull markets, and converting to cash at the onset of bear markets, gives greater returns over the long haul than a simple buy and hold strategy. Returns can be increased even more if we trade the downtrends either through put warrants or short selling.

The beginning of 1998 heralded the introduction of index warrants on the Australian Stock Exchange (ASX), with call and put warrants on the All Ordinaries Index and call warrants on the Gold Index. These index warrants offer great potential for trading and portfolio protection, as a purchase of call warrants gives profits in a rising market, while a purchase of put warrants gives profits when the market falls.

Index warrants (like equity warrants) have expiry times from around 9 months to 20 months when first introduced, so allow us to ride the medium-term and long-term uptrends and downtrends in the market.

The indices comprise a large number of stocks, so are insulated to some extent from sharp moves by individual stocks. Trading the index allows us to focus our attention on the market as a whole, which can be much less time-consuming than following the performance of a selection of individual stocks.

A variety of index-linked funds are also being introduced to the Australian market. These funds are designed to match the performance of particular indices very closely, and some have the added attraction of minimal fees.

The introduction of these new financial products makes it timely to look at analysis methods which are successful in picking the longer-term market trends. The methods discussed in this book comprise both technical and fundamental approaches. Technical analysis involves the use of technical indicators which usually require a computer for calculation. Fundamental analysis looks at the broader financial climate and need not involve computer calculations.

In my previous book, *Trading Stock Options and Warrants*, a number of technical indicators were discussed which are useful in finding trends in stocks. This present book is concerned with the medium-term trends in the stock indices, so discusses indicators appropriate to the market as a whole, rather than for individual stocks. We limit our analysis to a handful of tried and proven methods by drawing on the knowledge of respected writers and adapting these methods to the Australian stock market. The methods do not have to be complex, as top traders often use quite simple methods – what sets the winners apart from the losers is their understanding of risk and money management, and having the discipline to operate strictly according to their carefully worked out rules.

If we choose to trade index warrants using technical indicators, then our buy and sell signals are derived from an analysis of the All Ordinaries Index and the Gold Index. Similarly, if we trade an ASX industrials fund the buy and sell signals are derived from analysing the All Industrials Index. Consequently, we look at the performance of some popular technical indicators on these indices over the previous seven years, and so determine their reliability in the past, and consequently their potential for profitable trading in the future.

The technical indicators chosen are: moving averages, moving average convergence divergence (MACD), Coppock, advance/decline line, Turtle Trading and the Four Percent Model. The fundamental analysis includes Dow theory, interest rates and the Rule of 20.

For each of the indicators discussed the relevant maths is given, and also the code required to define the indicator in the charting software SuperCharts 4. An example of calculating the advance/decline line on the All Ordinaries Index using Ezy Charts software is also given.

Not all the indicators analysed show a pattern of profitable trading in the Australian market. Those that are unprofitable are included as a caution for the unwary, who may assume they must work on the stock indices just because they are included in many texts. It is hoped that the various methods of analysis discussed will stimulate the reader to explore these and other indicators of their own choosing, depending on their charting software and computing and analysis skills.

The topic of risk and money management is treated in some detail, as it is crucial to long-term success.

Most traders using technical indicators put considerable effort into deciding when to enter a trade, with less effort given to selecting the exit point. Successful traders do the opposite, so we pay particular attention to rules for closing technical trades.

INDEX FUNDS AND INDEX TYPE STOCKS

Index warrants offer a leveraged entry into the market, whereby if the index rises or falls say 5%, then the value of the warrant moves typically three times this amount. This is a two-edged sword, as profits are magnified, but so too are losses. Thus some investors may want to use the trading methods discussed to pick the trends, but not want the risk involved in warrants.

We look at some of the index-linked funds and the new Benchmark All Ordinaries Index Trust, and strategies for buying them during market uptrends. On downtrends the strategy may be to quit and stand out of the market, or hold and buy index put warrants to protect the value of a portfolio.

Short selling during downtrends is also investigated, along with the ASX rules to cover this practice.

The popular equity investment companies like Australian Foundation Investment Company, Argo Investments, Milton Corp and Templeton Global Growth Fund are found to be worthwhile buy and hold investments for long-term investors.

With the success of the Telstra float, a look at the floats over the past few years shows that the major new floats have performed exceptionally well. Where these companies also have call warrants on offer, the returns available are magnified even further.

THE OVER 50s

The new index warrants are useful in hedging retirement portfolios. The older person (who will be referred to as an "Over 50s") may adopt a variety of investment plans, and will usually have some assets in managed funds, where effectively a professional manager is paid to look after the assets. The performance of managed funds can vary greatly depending on the type of fund, and the competence of the management team. Unfortunately, funds can also go backwards in adverse financial times.

Depending on their background and interests, Over 50s may do some hands-on investing, either as a hobby to keep informed on the market, or more seriously to try to supplement the returns from their other investments. With the proliferation of media comment, finance magazines, brokers' research, books, and now the Internet, it is easy to be swamped by the data available, as well as being confused by the conflicting opinions expressed.

It is easy to lose sight of the forest for the trees, and the Over 50s' goal is to try to keep the nest-egg growing, no matter what the financial climate may be. A simple and usually profitable strategy is to invest in the major new floats and the better investment companies (and so gradually build up a blue chip imputed dividend portfolio), and to trade the index warrants and index-linked products. Such a strategy allows us to focus our attention on a small number of items, thus eliminating the need to monitor lots of individual stocks.

MUST I USE A COMPUTER?

Modern investors or traders have a personal computer and modem, which allows them to download stock exchange data each day from a data provider. Charting software is used to display the stock charts and to calculate and display a host of technical indicators, from which buy and sell decisions are made.

This can be off-putting to those without computing skills, or who do not want to be tied to their desk collecting and analysing data each day.

We discuss just a few of the popular technical indicators which are normally calculated by computer. We also give some methods of analysis which do not need a computer, but can be hand-calculated and easily applied to the small number of indices and investment companies of interest to us. Further, those methods involving fundamental analysis can be monitored with hand calculations.

Our prime interest is to pick the medium-term trends which typically run for anything from six weeks to nine months. Weekly and monthly data is used for analysis purposes, and calculations for finding signals need only be done each weekend. The Over 50s have a lot of living to do, and life is more enjoyable without the emotional distraction of being too close to the market each day.

HARDWARE AND SOFTWARE

Our results show a preference for the popular MACD indicator, plus having access to weekly bar charts of the indices. Some readers will already have a computer, software suite and data supplier, so they will be able to confirm the results listed in the following chapters, and monitor the indices with the MACD and various other indicators of their choosing.

However, for readers who want to set up a simple system at minimum cost, some suggestions are given in Chapter 31 on software packages and hardware to run these packages.

Of course it is necessary to have price data on the stocks and indices, and this data can be downloaded from a data supplier.

CUT-OFF DATE

There is always a time delay between finishing a manuscript and its publication. The manuscript of this book was finished in February/March 1998, so the charts and analysis cut off at this time.

In a work of this nature, it is the principles behind the analysis and the deductions from the analysis results which are important. The cut-off date should not affect this – in fact, the time period between the cut-off date and the reading of the book allows useful verification of the book's results and recommendations.

DISCLAIMER:

Readers should not act on the basis of any material in this book without considering (and, if appropriate, taking) professional advice with due regard to their own circumstances. The decision to trade, and the method of trading or investing is for the reader alone. Past performance is no guarantee of future profits.

Chapter 2

CHARTS OF SELECTED STOCK MARKET INDICES

WE START BY looking at the charts of some of the ASX indices, as an eyeball scan quickly shows if they have a pattern comprising well-defined uptrends and downtrends, which can lead to profitable trading. The charts selected are the All Ordinaries and the Gold Indices, which currently have index warrants available, and the All Industrials and All Resources Indices which are likely to have warrants available later.

Finally, charts are presented for the Dow Jones Industrial Average (DJIA), as we must always keep one eye on the US market, and have a good reason for taking a position contrary to the direction of its trend.

ALL ORDINARIES INDEX

At February 1998 the All Ordinaries Index comprised some 299 stocks from all sectors of the market. (For brevity the All Ordinaries Index will be shortened to AOI.) The AOI reflects the aggregate market value of all the covered stocks. However, it is market capitalisation weighted, which means that larger companies have proportionately more influence on the index than do smaller companies. Thus National Australia Bank comprises some 7% of the index, whereas scores of smaller companies comprise 0.1% or less.

All the ASX indices are market capitalisation weighted.

Figure 2.1 shows a monthly chart for the AOI going back to 1900. The ASX introduced a single national AOI in 1980, so the data in Figure 2.1 preceding this is calculated from the regional indices available at the time. The chart is drawn on a semi-log scale and has risen from about 10 points to 2800 points over 97 years, equating to an annual compound return of around 6.0%. In percentage terms, the crash in 1987 is seen to be comparable to the recession in the mid 1970s and the Great Crash in 1929. The dominant feature of the chart is that the index has climbed steadily since 1900, albeit punctuated by falls of varying severity.

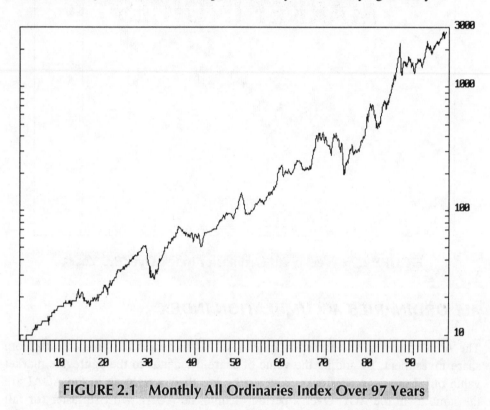

FIGURE 2.1   Monthly All Ordinaries Index Over 97 Years

Figure 2.2 overleaf shows the weekly price bar chart for the AOI for the 3.5 years from October 1994 to March 1998, also drawn on a semi-log scale. On this finer time scale, it is seen that the index has climbed from around 2000 to 2800 or 40%, giving an annual compound rate of around 10.0% over the 3.5 years. It is also worth noting that there are regular falls of over 100 points.

The AOI is the most important of the ASX indices as it covers the whole market. On the world scene, however, it is small stakes, as the Australian market comprises less than 2% of the total capitalisation of world equity markets.

For a stock to be included in the AOI it must satisfy specific rules regarding market capitalisation and liquidity. These rules are being tightened such that by 1 July 1998 the number of stocks in this index will be pruned to about 250.

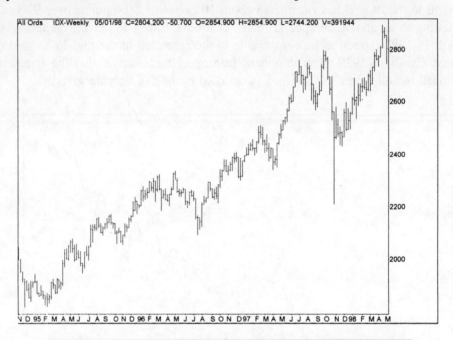

All Ords   IDX-Weekly   05/01/98 C=2804.200 -50.700 O=2854.900 H=2854.900 L=2744.200 V=391944

FIGURE 2.2   Weekly All Ordinaries Index Over 3.5 Years

ALL ORDINARIES ACCUMULATION INDEX

The All Ordinaries Accumulation Index (AOAI) measures the gross return from share investment, by adding the value of share dividends to the aggregate market value of all the covered stocks. The stocks and their weighting in the AOAI are the same as in the AOI. Over a period of time the AOAI will rise faster (or fall less) than the AOI.

Figure 2.3 opposite shows the AOAI and the AOI for the 18-year period from December 1979 to December 1997, starting from a common base of 1000. During this time the AOAI has risen to around 11000, giving an annual compound rate of 14.3%. Over the same period the AOI has risen to around 5000, for an annual compound rate of 9.3%.

The performance of managed funds is compared against the AOAI. Those funds which consistently out-perform this index are in demand by investors.

10

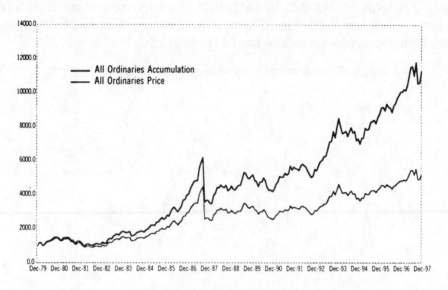

Source: *ASX Journal*

FIGURE 2.3   All Ordinaries Price and Accumulation Indices Over 18 Years

GOLD INDEX

At February 1997 the Gold Index comprised some 27 companies drawn from the Australian gold sector. Traditionally, holding gold has been a safe haven in times of high inflation and financial uncertainty, as the price of gold tends to rise at these times. However, during the Asian currency crisis of late 1997 gold continued to fall, reinforcing once again the fickleness of the financial markets, but also the complex relationship between the price of gold and the world economic system.

Gold is one of Australia's largest export earners, and the Gold Index reflects the price of gold and the health of this sector of the Australian economy. Figure 2.4 overleaf shows a weekly chart of the Gold Index spanning about nine years.

ALL INDUSTRIALS INDEX

At February 1998 the All Industrials Index comprised some 234 companies drawn from a cross-section of Australian manufacturers and service suppliers. As a group, these companies tend to be reasonably sedate in price behaviour in normal circumstances.

Figure 2.5 below shows the All Industrials Index spanning about eight years. From the low of under 2000 in 1991 the index has more than doubled to 4600 in 1998, giving an annual compound rate of around 11%.

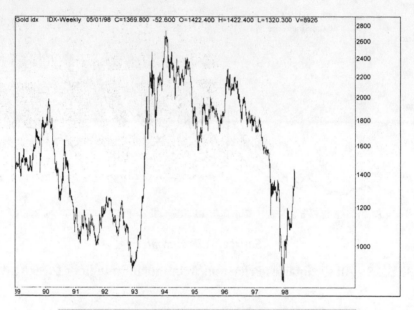

FIGURE 2.4   Weekly Gold Index Over 9 Years

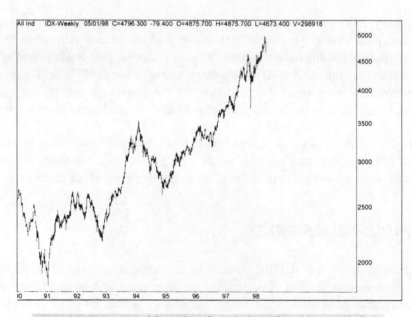

FIGURE 2.5   Weekly All Industrials Index Over 8 Years

ALL RESOURCES INDEX

At February 1998 the All Resources Index comprised some 65 companies drawn from a cross-section of Australian mining and energy industries. As a group, these companies tend to be volatile in price behaviour, being subjected to fluctuating global metal and commodity prices, and the economic cycle.

Figure 2.6 shows the All Resources Index spanning about nine years. From the low of 750 in 1989 the index doubled to 1500 in 1997, but has since lost half those gains due mainly to the Asian crisis and subsequent uncertainty in global demand for resources.

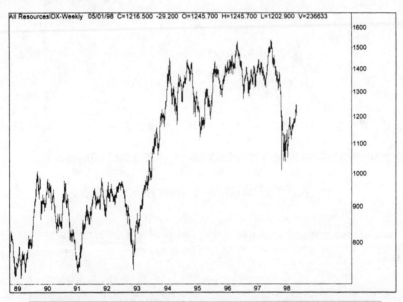

FIGURE 2.6   Weekly All Resources Index Over 9 Years

THE DOW JONES INDUSTRIAL AVERAGE

The DJIA comprises just 30 major stocks drawn from the prominent sectors of the US stock market, and is the international benchmark for index performance. The DJIA is price weighted, which means that the companies with higher-priced shares are more heavily weighted in the index.

The monthly plot in Figure 2.7 overleaf spans 97 years and shows that since the crash in October 1987, the DJIA has enjoyed a bull run of mammoth proportions, rising from around 2000 to over 9000 in 1998. In percentage terms this rise is equivalent to the run from 1949 to 1965. The only serious pull-back in

13

recent times occurred in the mini-crash of October 1997, but the index has since pushed on to new highs. It is interesting to note that from a low of 30 points in 1903 the DJIA has climbed to 9000 points in 1998, corresponding to an annual compound rate of about 6.0% – very similar to the AOI.

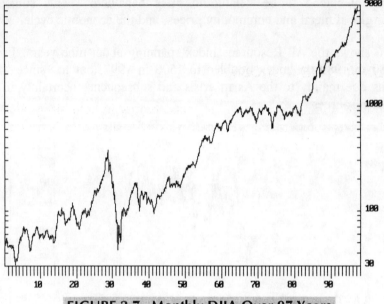

FIGURE 2.7   Monthly DJIA Over 97 Years

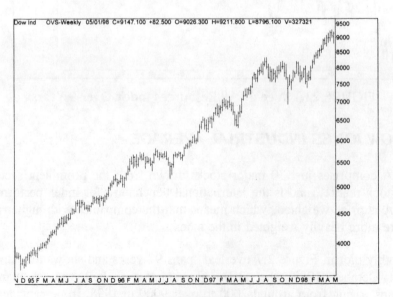

FIGURE 2.8   Weekly DJIA Over 3.5 Years

Figure 2.8 shows the weekly price bar chart for the DJAI for the 3.5 years from October 1994 to March 1998 drawn on a linear scale. On this finer time scale, it is seen that the DJIA is punctuated by regular small pull-backs. Comparison of Figures 2.1 and 2.7, 2.2 and 2.8 show that the timing of the trends in the Australian AOI closely match those in the DJAI, but the percentage magnitude of the trends may vary.

EYEBALLING THE INDICES

The purpose of trading an index is to make profits in both rising and falling markets, by using some trading vehicle that closely follows the behaviour of the index, and gives a monetary return akin to, or greater than, the percentage move in the index.

If an index rose gradually over a period of time with only very minor pull-backs, the trading plan could be nothing more than buy and hold quality stocks within that index. Alternatively, as a trader or investor looking for a greater percentage return, we could buy index call warrants and hold them to expiry.

However, markets are always adjusting upwards and downwards to real and perceived financial events. The market trends are somewhat arbitrarily defined as short-term (three to six weeks), medium-term (six weeks to nine months) and long-term (one to two years or longer).

Our primary concern is the medium-term, six week to nine month trends, as these offer profitable trading opportunities with index warrants.

All Ordinaries, All Industrials and All Resources Indices

Inspection of Figures 2.5 and 2.6 show the All Industrials Index and the All Resources Index march to the beat of a different drum.

Figure 2.1 shows the monthly AOI and, as discussed above, comprises stocks from both the industrial and resource sectors of the Australian market. It is of interest to note that the AOI is much more akin to the All Industrials Index than the All Resources Index. From the low of 1200 in 1991 the AOI more than doubled to 2800 in 1997. After the mini-crash in October 1997 the All Industrials has attained new highs. The AOI has partly recovered, but is being held back by the resource sector.

On a capitalisation basis, the AOI comprises about 70% industrial companies and 30% mining companies, so we would expect it to track the All Industrials Index fairly closely.

Figure 2.1 shows that within the AOI uptrends there are regular pull-backs of 150 points or more. This chart pattern is profitable from a trading point of view, provided we use a system that gets us onto each of the medium-term up and down legs, with a manageable number of whipsaws.

At March 1998 warrants are not available on the All Industrials Index, but if they are introduced some time in the future, they should give profitable trading opportunities.

Gold Index

Figure 2.4 shows the Gold Index has been in a steep downtrend since early 1996 as the price of gold has collapsed, partly due to selling of gold by world Central Banks to raise cash, and to meet European Union monetary conditions.

At the time of writing, only call warrants are available on the Gold Index. Over the past two years a purchase of put warrants on the Gold Index would have been very profitable. However, when the gold price rises some time in the future, the call warrants on the Gold Index should be a lively trading tool.

Chapter 3

SETTING THE GOALPOSTS

OUR FINANCIAL GOALS depend somewhat on our age, job prospects and job security, our financial commitments and lifestyle. Younger people with job security can afford to take greater risks in their trading and investing, as next month brings another pay cheque. The Over 50s, however, need to be careful in their preservation of capital.

Financial planning is always uncertain, but the goal is to achieve annual returns that grow at a faster rate than the Consumer Price Index (CPI).

Compound returns are calculated as:

$$S = P(1+r)^n$$

where:

P = the initial principal

S = the final sum

r = the annual compound interest rate expressed as a decimal, i.e. 8% = 0.08

n = the number of years

Similarly, if the principal P grows to an amount S in n years, the annual compound rate of return r is:

$$r = \text{antilog} \left(\frac{\log(S) - \log(P)}{n} \right) - 1$$

Table 3.1 shows the compound return for various annual rates and years of investment.

TABLE 3.1 Compound Interest Returns

Rate (% p.a.)	Years						
	1	2	3	4	5	7	10
5	1.05	1.10	1.16	1.22	1.28	1.41	1.63
10	1.10	1.21	1.33	1.46	1.61	1.95	2.59
15	1.15	1.32	1.52	1.75	2.01	2.66	4.05
20	1.20	1.44	1.73	2.07	2.49	3.58	6.19
25	1.25	1.56	1.95	2.44	3.05	4.77	9.31

This table shows that when investments grow at 5% p.a., then over 10 years they compound up to 1.63 times the initial investment. For investments to double in five years, an annual compound rate of 15% is required. Only the best managed funds achieve 15% or more growth a year with any consistency.

Both the investing and trading systems and strategies discussed in this book are aimed at producing above average returns on the money committed to them.

RULE OF 72

A quick method of calculating the compound rate required to double an investment is the Rule of 72 which states:

$$\text{Number of years to double} = \frac{72}{\text{annual compound rate}}$$

Thus an annual compound rate of 15% doubles investments in approximately $\frac{72}{15}$ = 4.8 years (cf. the correct value of 5.0 years in Table 3.1).

INVESTING SYSTEM GOALS

Chapter 23 discusses investment companies, while Chapter 24 discusses new floats. It is shown that the patient and discerning investor can achieve returns bettering 15% p.a. with these types of investments.

TRADING SYSTEM GOALS

When we look at technical trading systems there are literally scores to choose from. Some systems work best on futures, some on stocks and some on indices. Similarly, some systems work best with daily data, some with weekly and some with monthly data.

We are interested in the medium-term six week to nine month trends on the indices, which require weekly and monthly data to be used in calculating the indicator signals.

Stock market traders are a breed apart, who love the daily cut and thrust of the market and are organised to handle it. On the other hand, the Over 50s generally enjoy a simpler life, so the trading systems discussed here are selected with them in mind, though people of any age and market interest should find them useful.

Obviously the trading systems chosen must be profitable, but they must also be simple in concept and in operation. Only two or three trading systems need be monitored to pick the trading signals, and to confirm one another.

Thus the trading systems requirements are:

1. They must use only weekly or monthly close prices to give the entry and exit signals. Any analysis required can be done over the weekend and orders placed on Monday morning.

2. Where appropriate, stop orders can be left with the broker to quit a trade on predetermined profit or loss targets. Some brokers will only accept orders to sell at a particular price, while others cater for a variety of stop orders (see Chapter 6).

3. Wherever possible the trading systems must be mechanical, with clearly defined buy and sell signals, and with no need to search for elusive patterns within the charts.

4. It would be an advantage if some of the trading systems did not need a computer to do the calculations. Many Over 50s have a lifestyle which involves trips away from home. A pencil and paper system can be traded anywhere, whereas if a computer and price database is required, it may be necessary to either close positions before going away, or make guesses on incomplete information while away from home base. Alternatively, if we have a portable lap-top computer and modem, we can continue to receive data and do our analysis provided we have access to a phone outlet.

5. The system must be profitable trading index warrants or index-linked funds over a period of time. No system gives a profit on every trade, but over a one or two-year time frame, the system must deliver acceptable profits.

TRADERS

Successful traders are dedicated and disciplined in their pursuit of profits, and are likely to have arrangements in place to continue their trading when away from home base.

This may involve a mobile phone, a lap-top computer and a quotemaster to receive live price data. With this equipment they never need be out of contact with the market, and it is not a problem if the trading systems require a computer to perform the analysis and generate the buy and sell signals.

50% OF TRADES PROFITABLE

Successful traders use systems that are often right only 50% of the time, but which achieve a monetary profit-to-loss ratio of 2:1 or more.

Thus over 20 trades there are typically 10 wins for a profit of $10 \times 2 = 20$, and 10 losses for a loss of $10 \times 1 = 10$, giving a net profit of $20 - 10 = 10$.

One problem for the novice with a 50% system is that trades do not run in a neat profit, loss, profit, loss... sequence. After any trade, the next trade has an equal probability of being either a profit or a loss, and there can be strings of five or six consecutive losses or consecutive profits within a 50% system.

Our trading systems and strategies should achieve this 50% success rate with a profit-to-loss ratio of 2:1 or better. To cope with the strings of losses strict risk and money management rules must be adopted, which are discussed in Chapter 26.

BACK-TESTING

Back-testing is the term applied to running historic data through a technical system to determine its performance over the past, say, five or even ten years. Some technical systems have one or more parameters to adjust to match the system performance to the data, and this matching is called optimisation. (An example of optimising is the choice of the number of data to use in a moving average, e.g. 10-day, 20-day etc.)

If the trading system shows acceptable profits with little or no optimising during the back-testing, then we have confidence that it can be used profitably in the future.

Computer Analysis of the Futures Markets by LeBeau and Lucas gives an excellent discussion of back-testing various commodity markets using a variety of technical indicators.

In later chapters we apply a number of indicators to the AOI to demonstrate a variety of analysis techniques. Figure 3.1 shows the AOI as a monthly bar chart drawn on a linear scale. For back-testing purposes the data is partitioned into two segments. The first data segment is the 7.5 year period from August 1990 to March 1998. This segment is reasonably typical in so much as it contains a number of distinct uptrends and downtrends, as well as a sideways trading range during 1992. The data in this segment is analysed in later chapters with all the chosen indicators, and in some cases their performance is investigated using stops to increase the profitability. From this analysis the preferred methods of analysis for the AOI are selected.

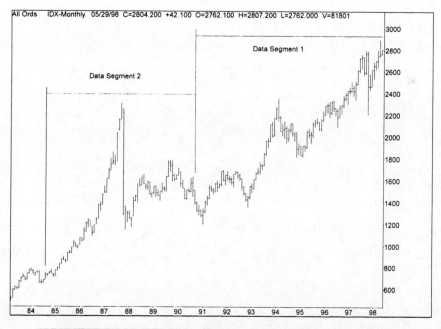

FIGURE 3.1   Monthly All Ordinaries Index Over 15 Years

The second data segment is the six-year period from mid-1984 to August 1990, which includes the crash of October 1987. The crash is deliberately excluded from the first data segment as it skews the results, particularly in analysing the effects of stops on profits. Any system which was short prior to the crash would show good profit results. Conversely, if the system was still long prior to the crash the results would be catastrophic.

The preferred analysis methods derived from the first data segment are applied to the second data segment in Chapter 16. The preferred methods are found to also work well on the second data segment, thus giving added confidence in their ability to work well in the future.

OTHER INDICES

Indices other than the AOI are analysed over a single segment of data spanning typically seven years. Readers with longer historic databases may like to analyse the indices over earlier time periods.

Chapter 4

SELECTING A TRADING SYSTEM

THE VARIOUS COMPONENTS of a trading system are:

1. Technical indicators to determine trading entry and exit signals.

2. Trading rules that define how to act on these signals.

3. Money management rules that define the level of financial risk involved in each trade.

In selecting a trading system it is prudent to follow the methods of successful traders who have proven track records over many years, and have handed down their expertise in their writings.

DR VAN THARP

Our first mentor is Dr Van Tharp, a research psychologist whose special interest is the psychology of winning in the markets. He counsels traders in methods of improving their trading and, over many years, his work has brought him in contact with top traders around the world. He has developed models of trading, covering particularly the psychological aspects of trading. He is a contributing editor for *Technical Analysis of Stocks and Commodities* magazine, and was interviewed in *Market Wizards* by Jack Schwager. Tharp has contributed three articles to the *Australian Technical Analysts Association* (ATAA) *Journal*, while one of his addresses to the ATAA is available on video.

As we progress in our reading and trading or investing, we move along the learning curve. Months or years down the track we come to realise that technical indicators are helpful but by no means infallible. The markets continue to develop yet more ways of fooling us, and the key to full understanding is tantalisingly still out of our grasp. We have a feeling that a piece of the jigsaw puzzle is missing, and that it has something to do with our temperament and the way we conduct our trading, rather than in finding the trading signals.

Tharp's writings are like a breath of fresh air blowing away much of the complex attitude we may have developed towards the market. He says that trading and investing are very simple processes which we human beings try to make into something much more complex. He considers there are just four trading rules:

1. Follow the trend.

2. Let the profits run.

3. Cut the losses.

4. Manage the money to stay in the game.

Readers will have seen these rules stated in numerous texts.

Tharp says that if a person follows these rules they will be successful in the markets. He recommends simplicity over complexity, with no more than two technical indicators and two filters being used in determining the entry and exit signals. (A filter is some set of logic which must be satisfied in conjunction with the technical indicator to confirm the indicator signal.)

Tharp firmly believes that far too much effort is put into finding the "best" entry point for a trade, whereas what is far more critical to the overall result is the logic and stops which are used to quit a trade. This topic is discussed further in subsequent chapters.

RICHARD DENNIS/RUSSELL SANDS

Our second port of call is to look at the methods of the "Turtle" traders. In 1983 Richard Dennis and Bill Eckhart entered into a bet as to whether successful trading could be taught. The term "Turtle" is applied to the people who were trained to decide the bet. Dennis was an exceptional trader who is reported to have traded $400 up to $200 million over some 20 years (or $4,000 up to $500 million, depending who is telling the story – either way an impressive feat). Russell Sands is one of the Turtles and, after becoming a successful trader, now writes and lectures on the Turtle methods.

One lecture Sands gave is recorded in the July 1997 *ATAA Journal*. He points out that their trading methods are intrinsically very simple, as their fundamental rule is to trade the trend. Their only technical indicator is that a rising price defines an uptrend, and a falling price defines a downtrend. This simple entry logic is backed up by strict and mandatory risk and money management rules, and filters to select the trades with a high probability of being profitable.

Sands does not try to pick the top or bottom of the trend, nor to predict how long or how far a trend will run – the trend is finished when prices confirm a move in the opposite direction. He stays with the trend till it turns, and is happy to extract 50% of the total trend in a trade.

Trading the trend means taking trades whenever the logic signals the start of a new valid trend, and consequently taking many trades where the trend does not develop into a major move in our direction. These wrong trades are exited at predetermined loss levels. Turtle trading gives a success rate of only 30% to 35%, but the successful trades capture the major legs in the markets, and more than compensate for the many small losses along the way.

It should be pointed out that Turtles trade the futures markets, where one or more commodity is usually moving strongly at any time. Much of their success lies in finding these strong moves, and ignoring the commodities which are listless. Further, the Turtles method uses aggressive pyramiding, i.e. when on a winning trend buying more contracts to increase the profits still more.

MARTIN ZWEIG/NED DAVIS

Martin Zweig is one of America's top analysts, and selected as the leading stock picker for two consecutive years by Hulbert's *Financial Digest*. He publishes a popular investment service, *The Zweig Forecast*, and provides research and investment strategies for associated firms managing over $500 million. In his book *Winning on Wall Street* Zweig presents a number of *simple, reliable and workable systems for playing – and beating – the stock market* (his words).

Zweig discusses two American stock indices which are weighted, viz. the New York Stock Exchange Composite (NYSE), and the Standard & Poors 500 (S&P

500). Also discussed are two unweighted indices, viz. the Value Line Index (VLI) and his own index, the ZUPI (Zweig Unweighted Price Index). An unweighted index gives equal weighting to all stocks, so is not dominated by changes in the price of the blue chip stocks. It should be noted that each of these indices apply to a broad basket of stocks traded on the New York Stock Exchange, in much the same way that there are different indices covering the major stocks on the ASX.

Futures contracts can be traded on each of the NYSE, S&P 500 and VLI, and Zweig presents several technical models to select buying opportunities. He too says "the trend is your friend" and all his models look for the start of strong rallies. One model uses the advance/decline ratio on the NYSE, while a second uses the ratio of up volume to down volume. He shows that the buying signals may occur only every couple of years, but the market then rises strongly for typically 12 months or more, while during the intervening times the market is flat, or trending down.

Zweig also presents a model developed by a colleague, Ned Davis, called the "Four Percent Model Indicator". This model takes the weekly close of the VLI, and a buy signal is given when the weekly close is 4% above the current trough. Similarly, a sell signal is given when the weekly close is 4% below the current peak. For the 19 years spanning mid-1966 to mid-1985 the model gave 84 legs, of which 50% were correct in determining the VLI trend. An initial investment of $1,000 would have grown to $176,000 at the end of the 19-year period. This growth is achieved by compounding the profits i.e. if the first trade was either up or down and gave a profit of 5%, then the starting value for the next trade is $1,050, etc. The growth is equivalent to an annualised return of about 16%. Over the same 19 years the VLI rose from around 130 points to 200 points but had a low of about 50 points along the way.

To capitalise on these moves, Zweig suggests trading futures on the VLI. For the more cautious he suggests that at the start of uptrends to buy American mutual funds which are weighted in favour of mid-cap stocks which comprise the VLI, and in downtrends to become partially or fully cashed up.

Zweig says the Four Percent Model could be modified slightly to work for weighted indices like the S&P 500, though it is not as successful as for the unweighted VLI and ZUPI.

The Four Percent Model gives impressive figures for a very simple trading system and is discussed more fully in Chapter 11, where it is applied to the AOI.

LESSONS FROM THE FOUR PERCENT MODEL INDICATOR

The Four Percent Model Indicator applied to the VLI illustrates several important points about trading the trend using mechanical systems, where trades are taken on each signal. Here, we will work through some of the maths, which will be used again in later chapters.

Zweig's figures show the details of the 84 trades spanning 19 years, which naturally comprise 42 buy signals and 42 sell signals.

For the buy signals:

20 were profitable, averaging a profit per trade of 15.3%

22 gave losses, averaging a loss per trade of -3.9%

$$\text{Net average profit} = \frac{(20 \times 15.3) - (22 \times 3.9)}{42} = 5.2\%$$

For the sell signals:

22 were profitable, averaging a profit per trade of 8.9%

20 gave losses, averaging a loss per trade of -3.6%

$$\text{Net average profit} = \frac{(22 \times 8.9) - (20 \times 3.6)}{42} = 2.9\%$$

For buy and sell signals:

$$\text{Average profit trade} = \frac{(20 \times 15.3) + (22 \times 8.9)}{42} = 11.9\%$$

$$\text{Average loss trade} = \frac{(22 \times 3.9) + (20 \times 3.6)}{42} = 3.8\%$$

Average profit/average loss = 3.1

$$\text{Average time per trade} = \frac{19 \times 52}{84} = 12 \text{ weeks}$$

$$\text{Average profit per trade} = \frac{11.9 - 3.8}{2} = 4.1\%$$

The points to note are:

1. Although the system is right for only 50% of trades, a satisfactory profit is achieved through the average profit/average loss ratio of 3.1, which in turn is made possible by letting the profits run.

2. Inspection of Zweig's results showed the longest winning streak was seven trades for a net gain of 82.8%, while there were two losing streaks of five trades for net losses of 11.9% and 14.0%.

PULLING THE THREADS TOGETHER

The above discussion highlights the fact that a trading system can be quite simple in concept yet still be profitable, provided it is based upon trend-following principles.

In following chapters we apply the MACD indicator, the Turtles method and the Four Percent Method to the AOI. Each is a trend-following method, and each gives potentially profitable results. We also look at stops to enhance profits, and filters to try to improve the various system performances.

The past few years have seen an exceptional bull run on the US markets which has spilled over to the Australian market. What the future holds is an open question, but if we trade with the trend we will be onboard the gravy train – and heading in the right direction.

Chapter 5

HEADS OR TAILS?

DR VAN THARP is emphatic that risk and money management strategies are much more important in generating trading profits than are the timing of entry points.

To illustrate this, he conducted a computer simulation of trading ten futures markets over a five-to-ten-year time span. He used the toss of a coin to enter the market, but strict risk criteria to quit a trade, and money management techniques to control the size of trades. The simulation shows profitable trading.

Tharp chose ten different commodities that were volatile, and consequently offered worthwile trading opportunities.

The basic rules were:

1. Initial kitty of $100,000 and a 1% risk value equating to $1,000. Trade parcel sizes where a $1,000 loss is a realistic figure given the volatility of that market.

2. Open a trade on the toss of a coin. If heads then assume an uptrend and open long; if tails assume a downtrend and open short.

3. Hold the trade until stopped out either by a profit exit on a winning trade, or stop-loss exit on a losing trade.

4. The profit exit for an up leg was a close price more than Y units below the leg peak (and the reverse for a down leg). The value of Y was chosen as a function of the commodity volatility over the past 10 days.

5. Quit the trade on a loss of $1,000.

6. Immediately open a fresh trade in the same commodity on the toss of a coin.

7. As the kitty grows increase the parcel sizes, and as the kitty shrinks decrease the parcel sizes.

It is apparent from the above rules that the entry is random, with a 50% chance of being right in picking the direction of the trend. The full simulation results gave only 38% profitable trades, as some potentially profitable trades were stopped out on leg pull-backs before the leg moved into profitable territory.

The system was successful overall because the profits were allowed to run, and the losing trades were ruthlessly quit.

Tharp's experiment is included here to emphasise again the golden rules of successful trading:

1. Follow the trend.

2. Let the profits run.

3. Cut the losses.

4. Manage the money to stay in the game.

Part II

TECHNICAL ANALYSIS

Chapter 6

MACD INDICATOR ON WEEKLY ALL ORDINARIES INDEX

IN MY PREVIOUS book *Trading Stock Options and Warrants*, a number of technical indicators were discussed which are useful in finding trends in stocks. This present book is concerned with the medium-term trends in the stock indices, so it discusses indicators appropriate to the market as a whole, rather than for individual stocks.

We start the analysis by looking at some popular technical indicators, and in later chapters investigate some fundamental methods. The maths required for the technical indicators is given in Appendix A.

The MACD is a popular and reliable indicator for both equities and stock indices, and was developed by Gerald Appel in 1979. The MACD is a trend-following system but has the advantage in that it picks the start earlier, and holds the trend longer, than many other trend-following indicators.

The mathematical treatment of the MACD is found in any book on technical indicators, and uses three exponentially smoothed averages (EMAs – see Appendix A). The 12-period and 26-period exponentially smoothed values are calculated, where the period may be days, weeks or months. The difference is obtained by subtracting the 26-period EMA from the 12-period EMA, and this is called the MACD line. The MACD line is now smoothed using 9-period exponential smoothing, and this smoothed line is called the signal line. The MACD line crosses up and down through the signal line, and the crossovers are taken as the start and finish of the stock trends. Thus, when the MACD line crosses above the signal line the trend is up, while when the MACD line crosses below the signal line the trend is down.

The MACD plot is usually constructed to show both the MACD line and the signal line, with the difference between them displayed as a histogram. Figure 6.1 shows the MACD indicator applied to the weekly AOI spanning 7.5 years, and it is seen that the indicator picks the major trends very well. The up arrows indicate buy signals and the down arrows indicate sell signals. The drawback to the MACD is one which is common to all trend-following indicators – when a stock or index is moving sideways, the indicator gives a series of signals which turn out to be whipsaws. (A whipsaw occurs when a new trend is signalled, but it quickly reverses so the indicator gives a signal to quit the trade at a loss. The trend then reverses again to its original direction, producing a second loss.)

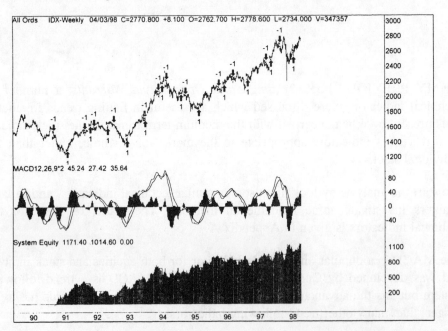

FIGURE 6.1   MACD on Weekly All Ordinaries Index Plus System Equity

BENCHMARK RESULTS

It is a simple matter to test the performance of the MACD on historic data using software like SuperCharts 4. The software has a "System Equity" facility which calculates all the buy and sell signals, and then tabulates the resulting trades in terms of profits and losses, with a summary table of overall profits, losses and relevant trading statistics. Further, the running tally of the profits from the trading legs can be plotted on the screen as shown in the bottom trace in Figure 6.1.

Figure 6.2 shows a trading leg with some terminology added. The notation TP in Figure 6.2 stands for "turning point", and is the time when a trade is opened or closed.

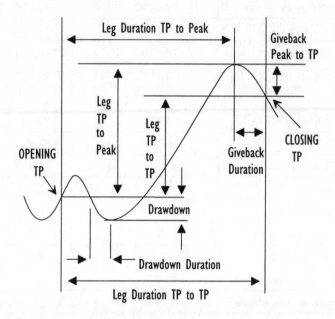

FIGURE 6.2 Trading Leg and Terminology

The 7.5 year time period from August 1990 to March 1998 has been chosen for analysing the AOI, and covers a number of uptrends and downtrends, as well as including the sideways trading range during 1992.

The MACD results on the weekly AOI are listed in the second column, titled 'Benchmark Result', in Table 6.1 overleaf. It is assumed that on each MACD signal the open trade is closed, and a new trade is opened in the opposite direction, i.e. there is always a trade open. For each trade SuperCharts 4 calculates the profit using the actual index weekly close prices, not the theoretical MACD trigger values. Further, SuperCharts 4 calculates the running profit up to the most recent *completed* trade. Thus the net profit value in Table 6.1 does not include a trade which is still open.

TABLE 6.1 Results For MACD on Weekly All Ordinaries Index

	Benchmark Result	250 Point Profit Target Stop
Open first trade	24/8/90	24/8/90
Opening index value	1469	1469
Close last trade	16/1/98	31/10/97*
Closing index value	2614	2416
Net profit	1014	1502
Gross profit	1796	2283
Gross loss	-782	-781
Number of trades	23	23
% profitable	52	52
Average profit trade	149	190
Average losing trade	-71	-71
Ratio avg. profit/avg. loss	2.1	2.7
Max. consecutive profits	2	2
Max. consecutive losses	4	4
Average weeks in profits	23	19
Average weeks in losses	10	10

*Last trade closed on 250 point profit target stop

Over the 7.5 years there are 23 trades averaging nearly four months per trade. During this time the AOI fell from 1469 points to about 1250 points before climbing to 2614 points, giving a net move of 1145 points or 78%. The MACD system gives a net profit of 1014 points over the same time, so is comparable to a "buy and hold" strategy.

However, the gross profit is 1796 points, so there is potential to increase the MACD performance if the gross losses can be reduced by using profit stops on the winning trades, and stop loss stops on the losing trades.

The values listed in column 2 of Table 6.1 are called the MACD Benchmark Result, and are displayed as a System Equity trace at the bottom of Figure 6.1.

STOPS TO IMPROVE RESULTS

There are various types of stops that can be used to improve trading profits. Three which can be easily applied using SuperCharts 4 are:

1. Profit target stops.

2. Dollar trailing stops.

3. Percentage profit trailing stops.

The purpose of each of these stops is discussed below, and applied to the MACD on weekly AOI. Note that SuperCharts 4 triggers all its stops on intra-day values, not on close of day or close of week prices. Figure 6.3 overleaf shows each of the stops applied to an up leg. The first diagram of each couplet shows the stop acting to increase the trade profit.

In the situations shown in the second diagram of Figure 6.3(a) and 6.3(c) the trade is quit using the normal indicator signal, and the stop has no effect on the trade. Lastly, the second diagram in Figure 6.3(b) shows how this stop can cause the trade to be quit prematurely at a reduced profit.

Stops and Stockbrokers

Most stockbrokers only accept buy and sell orders "at market" or at a fixed price. If we buy "at market" we accept the price being offered by the seller. Similarly, if we sell "at market" we accept the price being offered by the buyer.

If we give the broker an order to sell stock at a particular price which is above the market price, then the stock is only sold if the market rises to that price. Similarly, if we give the broker an order to buy stock at a particular price which is below the market price, then the stock is only bought if the market falls to that price.

If we choose to use profit target stops in a rising market, then we quit our holding when the price rises to a particular value. Any stockbroker can handle this type of order as it is a fixed price order.

However, if we choose to use dollar trailing stops or percentage profit trailing stops, then the broker needs to monitor the market to check if our stop value is reached, as we want to sell our position only if the price falls below the stop level. Using stops is the standard way of trading in futures markets, but not in the stock market. Consequently, most stockbrokers are not set up to monitor the market for clients at this level. However, all is not doom and gloom – the stockbroker Hogan & Partners (Hogan's) of Perth do handle dollar trailing stops and percentage profit trailing stops as a matter of course. Their phone number is (08) 9321 2366. Some other brokers also offer this facility, so it pays to shop around.

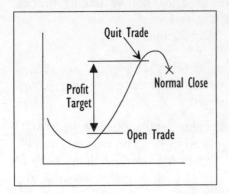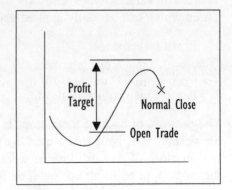

(a) Profit Target Stops

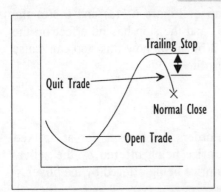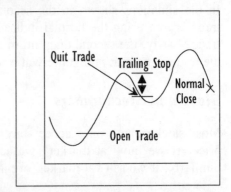

(b) Dollar Trailing Stops

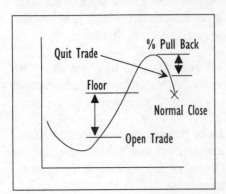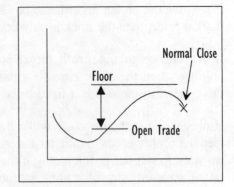

(c) Percentage Profit Trailing Stops

FIGURE 6.3   Trading Leg Stops

If our strategy is to trade the AOI using weekly data and stops, then if we deal with Hogan's, when we place the order to open a new trade we can also give instructions on the stop values to be applied. Hogan's will monitor the open position and close the trade as soon as possible after the stop is breached. Thus we can happily go about out daily golf or whatever, knowing that our trade is being looked after.

Conversely, if we use a stockbroker who does not accept stop orders other than fixed price orders, we can still use profit target stops, and these will be executed as soon as possible after the target value is achieved.

Profit Target Stops

Target stops are triggered when the leg achieves a predetermined amount. For the AOI this amount could be, say, 200 points. The rationale for using target stops is that with a trend-following system like the MACD, the exit signal is always given after the peak or trough has been passed (see Figure 6.2). By setting a target stop we hope to lock in a good profit before the leg turns over (but at the expense of aborting any very long and profitable legs).

If a profit target stop is set at 200 points, then when that profit is achieved the trade is closed, but a new trade is not opened until the next MACD signal is given. Alternatively, if the trade does not reach the target, then the trade is reversed on the next MACD signal. Figure 6.3(a) shows two trading legs with a target stop applied.

Table 6.2 overleaf shows the profit results for MACD on the weekly AOI for profit target stops ranging from 175 to 350 points. The time span is the same 7.5 years used in determining the benchmark results in Table 6.1.

In Table 6.2, the optimum value of the profit target stop is shown to be 250 points which produces a profit of 1502 points, and is 48% above the benchmark 1014 point value. It is encouraging to see in Table 6.2 that consistently improved profits above the benchmark are achieved over a band of profit target stops ranging from 200 points to 350 points, so the exact value of the stop is not critical.

The corresponding profit results obtained using the 250 point profit target stop are shown in the last column of Table 6.1. Inspection of the individual trades show there are seven instances where the trade is quit on the target profit stop, which mostly give a greater profit than would be achieved in waiting for the normal MACD signal on these trades.

The astute reader will see that there are some problems with profit target stops. Firstly, quitting a winning trade before it runs its course is contrary to Tharp's second rule. Secondly, the profit target stop is applied as an absolute amount, whereas a percentage of the opening value may be more logical. The reasons for starting the stop analysis with the profit target stop are:

- They are easy to understand.
- When optimised, these stops improve the net profit performance.
- SuperCharts 4 does not provide a percentage profit target stop.
- They can be executed by any stockbroker.

As a matter of interest, Hogan's will accept orders involving percentage profit target stops.

TABLE 6.2 MACD With Profit Target Stops on Weekly All Ordinaries Index

Stop (Points)	Profit (Points)	No.of Legs	% Right
None	1014	23	52
175	1192	23	52
200	1467	23	52
225	1412	23	52
*250	1502	23	52
275	1406	23	52
300	1288	23	52
325	1338	23	52
350	1388	23	52

*Optimum value of the stop

Dollar Trailing Stops

Dollar trailing stops are triggered when a trade moves a certain amount in the wrong direction. The trade is beginning to turn against us so we quit it, rather than wait for the MACD exit signal.

Suppose the trade reaches a profit of 124 points and then starts to retreat. If the dollar trailing stop is set at 50 points, then the trade is closed out when the profit falls to 74 points.

When the optimisation procedure for dollar trailing stops is run with stops between 50 and 200 points, we find that no stop value improves the benchmark result. This is somewhat surprising, but on checking the individual legs we find that several good profit legs are stopped out in pull-backs before the profit trend gets underway (see the second diagram in Figure 6.3(b)). These pull-backs are large enough to trigger the dollar trailing stops, but not severe enough to cause the MACD to close the leg. As noted earlier, the MACD holds a trend better than most of the trend-following indicators.

Percentage Profit Trailing Stops

Percentage profit trailing stops are triggered when a trade has moved into profit territory, but is beginning to retreat. (This is the stop used by Tharp in Chapter 5.) The percentage profit trailing stop exits the trade when the profit has retraced a preset percentage. To set the stop two parameters must be selected:

1. A "floor", which is the profit before the stop cuts in.

2. A percentage pull-back from this floor.

If the floor is set to 200 points, and the percentage to 10%, then the trade is closed out if the leg profit reaches at least 200 points and then retraces 10%, i.e. 20 points. A new leg is opened on the next MACD signal. Should the trade not reach 200 points, then the trade is quit on the next MACD signal. Figure 6.3(c) shows two cases of trading legs with a percentage profit trailing stop applied.

When the optimisation procedure for percentage profit trailing stops is run with the floor between 100 and 300 points, and the percentage between 5% and 30%, we find that the optimum result is a floor of 250 points and percentage value of 5%.

Table 6.3 shows the profit results for MACD on weekly AOI for percentage profit trailing stops with a floor of 250 points and the percentage ranging from 5% to 20%. The time span is the 7.5 years used previously.

TABLE 6.3   MACD With Percentage Profit Trailing Stops On Weekly All Ordinaries Index

Floor (Points)	%	Profit (Points)	No. of Legs	% Right
None		1014	23	52
*250	5	1770	23	52
250	10	1664	23	52
250	15	1558	23	52
250	20	1483	23	52

*Optimum value of the percentage pull-back

Table 6.3 shows that results well above the benchmark results are achieved for percentage pull-back values ranging from 5% to 20%. Further, the optimum profit of 1770 points is an improvement on the best value of 1502 shown in Table 6.2 for the profit target stops case. However, this result needs to be tempered with caution, as most of the improvement came from one exceptional trade in the mini-crash of October 1997, when the market collapsed and recovered within the span of one day.

Figure 6.4 shows the trading legs for the weekly AOI with the optimum percentage trailing profit stops added. The up and down arrows with the horizontal bar signify that the trade is stopped out prior to the MACD exit signal.

Some traders use a percentage profit trailing stop that changes in value as a function of the daily volatility of the stock or commodity being traded. When the volatility increases the stop size is increased, while when the volatility decreases the stop size is decreased. This approach ensures that when the stop is breached there is a high probability that the trend has reversed.

Variable stops calculated from daily prices are outside the scope of this book.

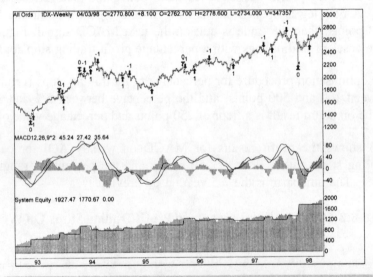

FIGURE 6.4   MACD On Weekly All Ordinaries Index With Percentage Profit Trailing Stops

Technical Stops

Many traders use technical stops to quit a trade. Inspection of price charts frequently shows horizontal bands of prices which are referred to as support and resistance levels. Figure 6.5 opposite shows a bar chart for the daily AOI, with the horizontal lines AB and CD defining a trading range. Suppose we open a down trade at X when the index breaks below the support line AB. The protective technical stop for this trade is placed just above CD, because if the index reverses and moves above CD it is likely to continue in that direction and so magnify our loss.

Support and resistance areas on a chart can be seen by eye, though some are clearer than others. Charting software does not automatically define support and resistance areas, so this method of quitting trades is not pursued in the text.

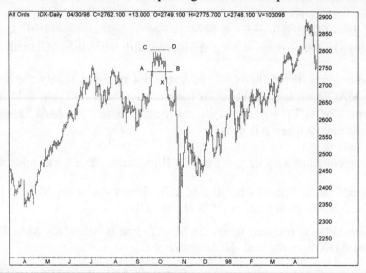

FIGURE 6.5   Daily All Ordinaries Index Showing Support & Resistance Lines

SLIPPAGE

Slippage is the term used to define the difference between a stop (or theoretical) value and the actual market value achieved. Suppose our weekend analysis shows the MACD indicator to give a buy signal with the AOI at 2607. Our trading rules are to open the trade early Monday morning, and the order is executed at, say, 2611, so the slippage is 4 points.

Slippage also includes brokerage, which always reduces the net profit. When analysis is performed on past data to compare different indicators it is customary to ignore slippage, as it introduces a variable encompassing an element of luck.

FILTERS TO IMPROVE RESULTS

To improve the performance of trend-following systems, it would be helpful to have some prior knowledge of which signals are likely to result in whipsaws, and which are followed by sustained trends. The Directional Movement Indicator (DMI) and Average Directional Movement Index (ADX) developed by Wells

Wilder are indicators which can provide this information, so they are often used as a filter to confirm or discard signals from other trend following systems. The mathematical details of the DMI and ADX are given in Appendix A.

When the ADX is rising it confirms the existence of either an uptrend or a downtrend. The ADX will normally start rising some time after the trend has begun. When used in conjunction with the MACD, an uptrend is confirmed when the MACD line is above the signal line *and the ADX is rising*. Similarly, a downtrend is confirmed when the MACD line is below the signal line *and the ADX is rising*. In either case, the leg is closed using normal MACD rules.

The second column (titled 'MACD') of Table 6.4 opposite shows the benchmark results for MACD on the weekly AOI (previously listed in Table 6.1), while the third column ('MACD +ADX') lists the results when the MACD signals are filtered using the 10-week ADX.

A more stringent filter also includes the DMI indicator. The logic rules are:

- An uptrend is confirmed when the MACD line is above the MACD signal line, the ADX is rising and +DI is above -DI.

- A downtrend is confirmed when the MACD line is below the MACD signal line, the ADX is rising and -DI is above +DI.

If a MACD signal occurs without a confirmation from the ADX and DMI, then any open trades are closed, but a new trade is not opened as the MACD signal is likely to be a whipsaw.

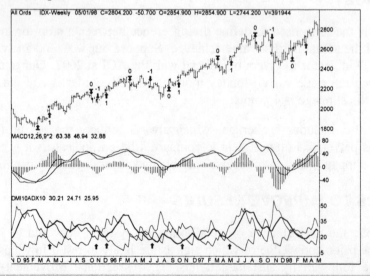

FIGURE 6.6   Weekly All Ordinaries Index With MACD and DMI/ADX Filter

The DMI and ADX are normally applied to daily data, but are also valid for weekly data. Figure 6.6 opposite shows the plot of the weekly AOI along with the MACD indicator and 10-week DMI and ADX indicators. The DMI comprises the +DI and -DI lines, while the heavy line in the bottom trace is the ADX indicator, and the up arrows mark some of the regions of rising ADX with complementing DMI logic. These regions are seen to coincide with well-defined price trends in the index chart.

Further, the upper trace of Figure 6.6 shows up and down arrows with horizontal bars, which signify that a trade has been closed using a MACD signal, while a new trade not opened at that time, but is waiting confirmation from the DMI and ADX logic.

The last column of Table 6.4 shows the results for the weekly AOI using MACD signals filtered using the 10-week DMI and ADX signals. For each set of results in Table 6.4, no stops are used and the time span is the 7.5 years used previously.

TABLE 6.4   Results For Weekly All Ordinaries Index With MACD & Filters

	MACD	MACD + ADX	MACD + DMI/ADX
Open first trade	24/8/90	28/9/90	28/9/90
Opening index value	1469	1397	1397
Close last trade	16/1/98	16/1/98	16/1/98
Closing index value	2614	2614	2614
Net profit	1014	892	594
Gross profit	1796	1216	1018
Gross loss	-782	-324	-424
Number of trades	23	20	18
% profitable	52	65	56
Average profit trade	149	93	101
Average losing trade	-71	-46	-53
Ratio avg. profit/avg. loss	2.1	2.0	1.9
Max. consecutive profits	2	3	3
Max. consecutive losses	4	2	3
Average weeks in profits	23	18	19
Average weeks in losses	10	7	9

Table 6.4 shows that the ADX filter used by itself eliminates three trades and increases the number of winning trades to 65%, but reduces the net profit. The combined DMI/ADX filter eliminates five trades and reduces the size of the average losing trades. However, in this case trades are opened later through waiting for the DMI/ADX logic to be satisfied, resulting in smaller profits from the winning trades.

From these results it is concluded that neither the ADX nor the DMI/ADX filters are particularly helpful in increasing the overall profitability of the MACD on weekly AOI.

STRATEGY FOR MACD ON WEEKLY ALL ORDINARIES INDEX

The above discussion shows that the trend-following MACD system gives reasonable results on the weekly AOI. These results are substantially improved when a target stop is used.

Suggested trading rules are:

1. Use the standard MACD(12,26,9) index on weekly close data.

2. The target profit stop is 250 points.

3. Open trades on the MACD signal. Analysis is done on the weekend, and orders will usually be placed on Monday mornings.

4. Close trades when the target profit is reached on an intra-day basis, or on the next MACD signal, whichever is sooner. Any stockbroker can execute a fixed price order which is effectively a profit target stop.

5. If the trade is closed on a target profit stop, wait for the next MACD signal to open the next trade.

The results of Table 6.1 show that the MACD with profit target stops set to 250 points on the weekly AOI gives a profit of 1502 points over 7.5 years to January 1998.

Chapter 16 takes up the MACD on weekly AOI again, and discusses the percentage returns available in trading index warrants using this system.

Chapter 7

MACD ON DAILY & MONTHLY ALL ORDINARIES INDEX

WEEKLY DATA IS our preferred time frame, but some of the indicators discussed later are specifically intended for either daily or monthly data. Thus results are calculated for the MACD on the AOI with these time frames for comparative purposes.

MACD ON DAILY ALL ORDINARIES INDEX

Column 2 ('MACD') of Table 7.1 overleaf lists the results for MACD on daily AOI over the 7.5 year period from July 1990 to January 1998. The starting and ending dates are selected so as to overlay the weekly trades from Table 6.1 as closely as possible.

Column 3 of Table 7.1 lists the results using a 14-day DMI/ADX filter. No stops are used in either case.

Table 7.1 shows that the MACD indicator applied to the daily AOI gives numerous trades (166) over the 7.5 years, but only 34% are profitable, and the net profit is just 113 points. The MACD gives a tantalisingly high gross profit of 3400 points, but surrenders most of it in whipsaws.

When 14-day DMI/ADX is used as an entry filter the number of trades drops to 103, but makes little difference to the net profit or the percentage of winning trades.

TABLE 7.1   Results For Daily All Ordinaries Index With MACD And DMI/ADX Filter

	MACD	MACD + DMI/ADX
Open first trade	24/7/90	17/9/90
Opening index value	1587	1543
Close last trade	12/1/98	12/1/98
Closing index value	2542	2542
Net profit	113	226
Gross profit	3400	1970
Gross loss	-3287	-1744
Number of trades	166	103
% profitable	34	37
Average profit trade	60	51
Average losing trade	-29	-26
Ratio avg. profit/avg. loss	2.0	1.9
Max. consecutive profits	3	4
Max. consecutive losses	13	7
Average days in profits	21	18
Average days in losses	7	6

For the MACD case, when profit target stops are applied ranging from 60 to 200 in steps of 20 points, the optimum result is a stop value of 120 points, giving a net profit of 417 points.

We conclude that the daily AOI is too volatile and whippy to give satisfactory results with the trend following MACD indicator.

MACD ON MONTHLY ALL ORDINARIES INDEX

Table 7.2 opposite lists the results for the MACD indicator on monthly AOI. The results in column 2 are for MACD, while the results in the column 3 are using an optimum profit target stop of 125 points. The time span is again adjusted to cover the 7.5 years used previously.

TABLE 7.2   Results For Monthly All Ordinaries Index With MACD And Profit Target Stop

	MACD	125 Point Profit Target Stop
Open first trade	30/3/90	30/3/90
Opening index value	1535	1535
Close last trade	28/11/97	28/2/97*
Closing index value	2465	2475
Net profit	80	706
Gross profit	555	875
Gross loss	-475	-169
Number of trades	8	8
% profitable	50	88
Average profit trade	138	125
Average losing trade	-118	-169
Ratio avg. profit/avg. loss	1.2	0.7
Max. consecutive profits	1	6
Max. consecutive losses	2	1
Average months in profits	13	4
Average months in losses	10	3

*Last trade closed on 125 point profit target stop

Table 7.2 shows the MACD with a profit target stop of 125 points applied to the monthly data gives just eight legs over the 7.5 year span, but with an 88% success rate. The net profit is 705 points, which again is well down on the preferred weekly results of 1502 points.

Chapter 8

MOVING AVERAGES ON WEEKLY ALL ORDINARIES INDEX

MOVING AVERAGES HAVE been around for centuries, and have stood the test of time because they are both reliable and simple to understand and to calculate.

Moving averages are trend-following indicators. For a 10-week close price single moving average (SMA) the last 10 weekly close prices are added and divided by 10, with the resulting value being this week's average.

Trading signals with moving averages are given in a variety of ways, but the resulting signals define the start and end of a price trend. The maths for the various moving averages discussed in the text are given in Appendix A.

SINGLE MOVING AVERAGE

To determine the medium-term trends with a SMA a long time interval is used, typically 20 to 30 weeks (or 150 to 200 days). Figure 8.1 opposite shows the weekly close price of the AOI along with a 20-week SMA on the close price data.

The trading rules are:

1. An uptrend is signalled when the close price crosses upwards through the SMA.

2. A downtrend is signalled when the close price crosses downwards through the SMA.

3. On each signal close existing trades and open new ones in the reverse direction.

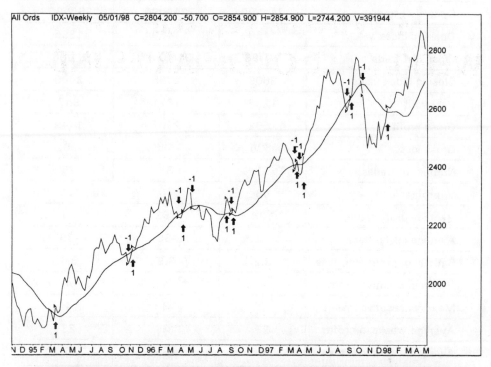

All Ords   IDX-Weekly   05/01/98 C=2804.200 -50.700 O=2854.900 H=2854.900 L=2744.200 V=391944

FIGURE 8.1   Weekly All Ordinaries Index With 20-Week SMA

Using SuperCharts 4 we optimise the SMA period over the range 20 to 30 in steps of 2 weeks, and find the optimum value to be 20 weeks. Column 2 of Table 8.1 overleaf shows the results for the 20-week SMA on the weekly AOI over the 7.5 year time span used in Table 6.1.

Table 8.1 shows that the 20-week SMA net profit of 1255 points is higher than the 1014 points for the MACD shown in Table 6.1, but notice that the SMA produces 31 legs with 48% correct compared to the MACD values of 23 and 52%. If we now apply the profit target stop the optimum value is again found to be 250 points, and the net profit is increased to 1670 points. These optimum values are shown in column 3 of Table 8.1.

TABLE 8.1 Results For 20-Week SMA On Weekly All Ordinaries Index

	SMA	250 Point Profit Target Stop	Filter X = 0
Open first trade	24/8/90	24/8/90	28/9/90
Opening index value	1469	1469	1395
Close last trade	2/1/98	31/10/97	2/1/98
Closing index value	2609	2395	2609
Net profit	1256	1671	947
Gross profit	1892	2307	1449
Gross loss	-636	-636	-502
Number of trades	31	31	25
% profitable	48	48	48
Average profit trade	126	153	120
Average losing trade	-39	-39	-39
Ratio avg. profit/avg. loss	3.2	3.9	3.1
Max. consecutive profits	4	4	4
Max. consecutive losses	3	3	4
Average weeks in profits	23	16	23
Average weeks in losses	3	3	5

It is not recommended to use the SMA by itself for trading purposes. A simple filter that is often used with the SMA is to wait for the SMA to turn over a specific amount before confirming the trade. The first signal marked A in Figure 8.1 is an up signal but occurs while the SMA is still moving downwards. To use the filter we would wait a couple of weeks for the SMA to turn upwards. Similarly, the second signal marked B in Figure 8.1 is a down signal but occurs while the SMA is still moving upwards.

If we set the filter such that the SMA must turn around say X points, then the trading rules become:

1. An uptrend is signalled when the close price has crossed upwards through the SMA, *and the SMA has moved X points or more up from its trough.*

2. Quit the trade when the close price crosses below the SMA.

3. A downtrend is signalled when the close price has crossed downwards through the SMA, *and the SMA has moved X points or more down from its peak*.

4. Quit the trade when the close price crosses above the SMA.

Suppose we use a filter with $X = 0$, i.e. the SMA has either bottomed out or topped out. The results for the 20-week SMA with this filter over the same 7.5 years of weekly AOI are shown in column 4 of Table 8.1. The number of trades has fallen to 25 while the percentage correct remains at 48%, and the net profit has fallen to 947 points.

DOUBLE MOVING AVERAGE

The moving average concept can be extended to double and triple moving averages.

The double moving average (DMA) comprises a shorter duration SMA and a longer duration SMA. Figure 8.2 overleaf shows a 5-week and 20-week SMA applied to the weekly AOI. An uptrend is signalled when the 5-week SMA crosses above the 20-week SMA, while a downtrend is signalled when the 5-week SMA crosses below the 20-week SMA. These crossover points are quite clearly seen in Figure 8.2, and it is apparent that the crossovers occur 3 to 6 weeks after the peak or trough of the price data. This delay may be reasonable for opening the trade, as it gives time for a valid trend to develop. However, when closing the trade the delay means the leg peak/trough is well past before the signal to quit is given. This in turn means some of the leg profit is given up before the trade is closed.

SuperCharts 4 allows us to optimise the number of periods in both the moving averages. Thus we select the short duration SMA value to take the values 1 to 11 in steps of 2, and the longer duration SMA to take the values 15 to 40 in steps of 5. When all these DMA combinations are applied to the weekly AOI over the same 7.5 year period used previously, none gives better results than the 20-week SMA discussed above.

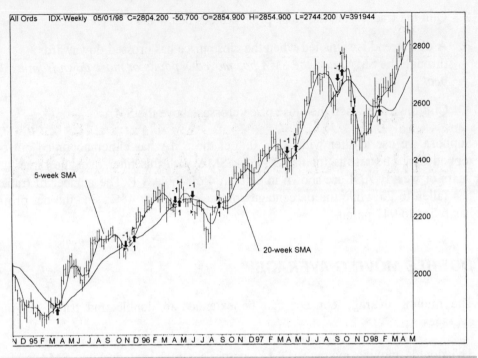

FIGURE 8.2 Weekly All Ordinaries Index With 5-Week And 20-Week DMA

TRIPLE MOVING AVERAGE

The triple moving average (TMA) uses one pair of SMAs to open a trade, and a second, more agile, pair of SMAs to close the trade, in an attempt to overcome the disadvantages of DMAs noted above. TMAs are discussed in the next chapter.

Chapter 9

TRIPLE MOVING AVERAGE ON DAILY ALL ORDINARIES INDEX

IT IS OF INTEREST to determine the results of moving averages on daily All Ordinaries Index data to see how they compare with the MACD results from Chapter 7.

The TMA indicator uses one pair of SMAs to open a trade, and a second, more agile, pair of SMAs to close the trade.

BASIC TMA

The three SMAs can be combined in several ways and also have various periods. One method, which we will call "Basic TMA", uses the popular values of 4-day, 9-day and 18-day for the SMAs.

The trading rules for the Basic TMA are:

1. An uptrend is signalled when the 9-day SMA crosses above the 18-day SMA.

2. Quit the trade when the 4-day SMA crosses below the 9-day SMA.

3. A downtrend is signalled when the 9-day SMA crosses below the 18-day SMA.

4. Quit the trade when the 4-day SMA crosses above the 9-day SMA.

Column 2 of Table 9.1 shows the results obtained using this Basic TMA on daily AOI over the 7.5 years discussed previously.

TABLE 9.1   Results For Daily All Ordinaries Index With TMA And DMA

	Basic 4,9,18 TMA	9,18 DMA	Advanced 4,9,18 TMA
Open first trade	31/7/90	30/3/90	31/7/90
Opening index value	1573	1535	1573
Close last trade	12/1/98	30/12/97	12/1/98
Closing index value	2542	2601	2542
Net profit	355	382	671
Gross profit	1658	2578	2686
Gross loss	-1303	-2196	-2015
Number of trades	100	99	148
% profitable	44	34	44
Average profit trade	37	75	41
Average losing trade	-23	-33	-24
Ratio avg. profit/avg. loss	1.6	2.2	1.7
Max. consecutive profits	6	3	3
Max. consecutive losses	6	9	6
Average days in profits	11	33	13
Average days in losses	5	12	5

Once again, Table 9.1 shows that daily data produces a high number of trades (100) but with a net profit of only 355 points. The average profit trade is just 37 points and lasts typically 11 days. These small values are a result of the agile 4,9-day SMA exit logic.

As a matter of interest, results are also obtained without this exit logic, i.e. eliminating the active 4-day SMA and effectively becoming a double moving average (DMA). The trading rules are now only items 1 and 3 above. The results are shown in column 3 of Table 9.1 (labelled '9,18 DMA'). The resulting net profit is much the same at 382 points, the average profit trade is much better at 75 points, but the percentage of profit trades has fallen to 34%.

ADVANCED TMA

An alternative TMA method, which we will call "Advanced TMA", has slightly different entry and exit logic. Using the same values of 4-day, 9-day and 18-day for the averages, the trading rules for the Advanced TMA are:

1. An uptrend is signalled when the 4-day SMA is above the 9-day SMA, *and* the 9-day SMA is above the 18-day SMA.

2. Quit the trade when the 4-day SMA crosses below the 9-day SMA.

3. A downtrend is signalled when the 4-day SMA is below the 9-day SMA, *and* the 9-day SMA is below the 18-day SMA.

4. Quit the trade when the 4-day SMA crosses above the 9-day SMA.

Column 4 of Table 9.1 shows the results obtained using this triple moving average on daily AOI over the 7.5 years discussed previously.

Figure 9.1 shows the logic rules for both the Basic TMA and Advanced TMA applied to an uptrend. The salient features of the trend are marked A, B, C, D, E and F. The trend begins at B for both the Basic TMA and the Advanced TMA, with the 9-day SMA crossing above the 18-day SMA. (The 4-day SMA has already crossed the 9-day SMA at A.)

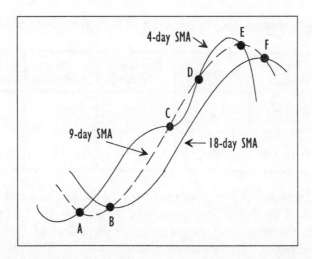

FIGURE 9.1   Schematic Of Logic Rules For Basic And Advanced TMA

At C the 4-day SMA crosses below the 9-day, thereby closing the up trade for both the Basic TMA and the Advanced TMA. At D the 4-day SMA moves back above the 9-day SMA, thereby opening a new up trade in the Advanced TMA, but not the Basic TMA. This trade is closed at E.

Finally, at F the conditions are right for both the Basic TMA and Advanced TMA to open a down trade.

Referring to Table 9.1 we see, as expected, that the Advanced TMA produces more trades (148) compared to 100 for the Basic TMA. However, the ratio of average profit/average loss is substantially the same in both cases, so the more sophisticated Advanced TMA is not really any better than the Basic TMA in this case.

OPTIMISING SMA PERIODS

The literature on moving averages contains varying preferred SMA values to use in TMAs. All are probably correct for the particular stock, index or commodity being analysed, at a particular time. It is a big ask for a single set of values to always be best in all cases.

The optimising facilities in SuperCharts 4 can be used to find the three SMA values which give maximum profit on the daily AOI over our 7.5 year analysis period. For the Basic TMA the SMA values are 5,11,14, while for the Advanced TMA the values are 5,12,20. Table 9.2 lists the more important parameters from the analysis.

TABLE 9.2 Optimum Results For Daily All Ordinaries Index With TMA

	SMA Values	Net Profit	Number of Trades	% Profitable	Ratio Avg. Profit/Avg. Loss
Basic TMA	5,11,14	1069	144	49	1.7
Advanced TMA	5,12,20	992	103	46	2.0

Optimising has increased the net profit for both the Basic TMA and the Advanced TMA. Inspection of the optimising results (not shown) reveals that the net profit is fairly sensitive to the three SMA values chosen. Comparison of Tables 9.1 and 9.2 show that the number of trades varies considerably with the SMA values chosen.

We conclude that the daily AOI is too volatile and whippy to allow profitable trading with either the Basic TMA or the Advanced TMA.

Chapter 10

TURTLE TRADING ON DAILY ALL ORDINARIES INDEX

CHAPTER 4 INTRODUCED the Turtles and pointed out that their philosophy is to follow the trends, and that trends continue until the price behaviour signals the end of the trend by reversing. The rules that the Turtles talk about are very simple, but their complete trading system is much more complex, requiring various filters to select the best trades, the pyramiding of winning trades, and strict stops to quit losing trades.

The simple rules are:

1. A new uptrend is defined on a new 20-day high, and the trend continues until there is a 10-day low.

2. A new downtrend is defined by a new 20-day low, and the trend continues until there is a 10-day high.

A new 20-day high means that today's price is higher than the price 20 days ago, but also higher than all the intervening days. The highs and lows may be confined to closing prices, or alternatively they could be drawn from intra-day values.

The above rules show that more confirmation is required to open a trade, than to close it. Stated another way, Turtles close a trade when the trend starts to falter, and then wait for confirmation of the new trend before opening the next trade.

TURTLE MODEL APPLIED TO DAILY ALL ORDINARIES INDEX

We now apply the principles of the Turtle Model to the daily AOI. The intra-day high and intra-day low values are used. Table 10.1 lists the profit performance for the 7.5 year time span used previously.

TABLE 10.1 Results For Daily All Ordinaries Index With Turtle Trading

Open first trade	21/8/90
Opening index value	1552
Close last trade	12/1/98
Closing index value	2542
Net profit	638
Gross profit	2214
Gross loss	-1576
Number of trades	80
% profitable	41
Average profit trade	67
Average losing trade	-33
Ratio avg. profit/avg. loss	2.0
Max. consecutive profits	4
Max. consecutive losses	8
Average days in profits	28
Average days in loss	10

Table 10.1 shows the simple Turtle Model gives a profit of 637 points for the 7.5 year time span analysed, and produces 80 trades. These results are slightly better than for MACD or moving averages on daily data as listed in Tables 7.1 and 9.1 respectively, although they are still far short of the MACD on weekly data using profit target stops.

As mentioned previously, Turtle Trading involves the use of stops to protect profits and cut losses. We can test some of the optimisation possibilities using SuperCharts 4.

Firstly, we optimise the number of days in the opening and closing sequences to trigger a signal. Setting the opening values to the range 15 to 29 in steps of 2 days, and the closing values to the range 5 to 13 in steps of 2 days, it is worth noting that the optimum values are 19 and 9. These are the values used by the Turtles and correspond to the 20-day open and 10-day closing rules (see Appendix A).

Secondly, if we optimise the profit target stop in the range 100 to 400 in steps of 25 points, there is no noticeable improvement in profit.

Lastly, we optimise the dollar trailing stop in the range 25 to 200 points in steps of 25 points. With the stop set at 25 points the profit rises to 1051 points, but the number of trades doubles to 162. (An up trade, say, can be stopped out on a 25 point pull-back, but a new high will open another up trade, etc.)

Chapter 11

FOUR PERCENT MODEL

THE FOUR PERCENT Model is included because of its simplicity, and its proven performance on the American market. All that is required is the weekly close of the Value Line Index which can be obtained from the SBS TV *Business Report* on Saturday morning, or from most stockbrokers and futures brokers, or the Internet.

APPLIED TO VALUE LINE INDEX

The Four Percent Model was discussed briefly in Chapter 4, where it was shown that when applied to the unweighted American Value Line Index over the 19-year time period from 1966 to 1985, it generated an annual return of about 16%, which is much larger than the annual return on the VLI over the same period of only 2%.

I have applied the Four Percent Model to the VLI over the 5.5 year time frame from November 1992 to March 1998. The results are listed in Table 11.1. A weekly chart of the VLI over these 5.5 years is shown in Figure 11.1 overleaf, drawn on a linear scale. During the 5.5 year

TABLE 11.1 Results For Weekly VLI With Four Percent Model	
Open first trade	6/11/92
Opening index value	251
Close last trade	20/3/98
Closing index value	490
Net profit	162
Gross profit	211
Gross loss	-49
Number of trades	13
% profitable	69
Average profit trade	23
Average losing trade	-12
Ratio avg. profit/avg. loss	1.9
Max. consecutive profits	3
Max. consecutive losses	1
Average weeks in profits	27
Average weeks in losses	9

span the VLI has risen from around 250 to 490 points or 96%, which equates to an annual rate of 13%.

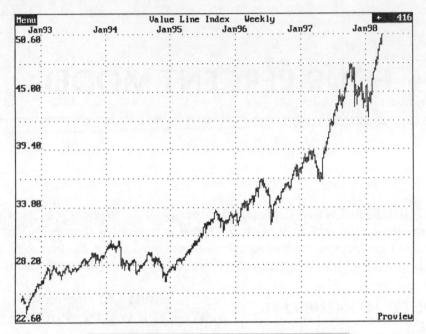

FIGURE 11.1 Weekly VLI Over 5.5 Years

When the 13 trading legs are expressed in terms of percentage profits and losses (not shown in Table 11.1), the average percentage trade is 3.9% and the annual percentage return is 9%. The average leg length is now $\frac{5.5 \times 52}{13}$ = 22 weeks. Chapter 4 lists the average profit per trade on earlier data as 4.1% with average leg length of 12 weeks, producing an annual return as 16%. Thus the Four Percent Model is continuing to give similar profits per trade, but now the leg durations are longer, resulting in lower, but still acceptable, profits on the VLI.

PERCENT MODEL APPLIED TO WEEKLY AOI

We now apply the principles of the Four Percent Model to the weekly AOI, to find the percentage value which gives the best profit. Table 11.2 opposite lists the profit performance against the percentage value, for a time span of 7.5 years used in previous chapters.

All the results for the Percent Model on the VLI and AOI have been done on a custom-built program, as SuperCharts 4 does not have the facility to construct an indicator that picks peaks and troughs accurately. However, an approximation to the Four Percent Model which can be generated in SuperCharts 4 is given in Appendix A.

TABLE 11.2 Weekly All Ordinaries Index And Various Percentage Values

%	2	2.5	3	3.5	4	4.5
Net profit	1028	938	664	1353	977	660
Gross profit	2594	2383	2257	2486	3159	1983
Number of trades	62	52	46	32	30	28
% profitable	45	46	41	47	47	43

Table 11.2 shows that as the percentage value increases from 2% to 4.5%, the number of trades falls, but the success rate remains fairly constant at around 46%. Balancing a large net profit against a small number of trades, the optimum value for the percent is 3.5%. This approach is called the 3.5 Percent Model in this book. Table 11.3 shows the full set of trading values for the weekly AOI with the 3.5 Percent Model.

The 3.5 Percent Model results are very similar to the MACD benchmark results from Table 6.1. The 3.5 Percent Model net profit is 1353 points, and the last trade closes on 20/3/98, whereas the benchmark net profit is 1014 points and the last trade closes on 16/1/98. The extra trade in the 3.5 Percent Model gives a profit of 210 points, so without this trade the net profit falls to 1143 points. The benchmark result is achieved with 23 trades, while the 3.5 Percent Model result comes from 32 trades, so taking into account brokerage charges, the benchmark result is superior.

Chapter 6 shows that profit target stops improve the benchmark result. However, profit target stops are not really applicable to the 3.5 Percent Model, as this model relies upon the trades running their full course, and then quitting on a 3.5% reversal.

TABLE 11.3 Results For Weekly All Ordinaries Index With 3.5 Percent Model

Open first trade	27/7/90
Opening index value	1578
Close last trade	20/3/98
Closing index value	2767
Net profit	1353
Gross profit	2486
Gross loss	-1133
Number of trades	32
% profitable	47
Average profit trade	166
Average losing trade	-67
Ratio avg. profit/avg. loss	2.5
Max. consecutive profits	3
Max. consecutive losses	4

*　　*　　*　　*　　*　　*　　*

The simplicity and success of the Four Percent Model applied to the VLI demands that we explore a few more avenues before giving it up. Chapter 12 looks at the close correlation between the American market and the Australian market, and uses signals from the VLI for the Australian market.

Chapter 12

CORRELATION BETWEEN THE VLI & THE ALL ORDINARIES INDEX

NEW YORK IS the home of the world's leading stock market, where the benchmark index is the DJIA, even though it contains just 30 stocks. There is an old saying that when the Dow sneezes the rest of the world catches a cold. It is true that the New York markets set the world scene, though the stock markets of individual countries also move in response to internal conditions and circumstances.

There is a definite correlation between the Australian market and the American market, as can be seen by looking at the monthly charts of the AOI and the DJIA shown in Figures 2.1 and 2.7. The shorter time span charts, Figures 2.2 and 2.8, show that the DJIA has risen strongly in the past 3.5 years, while the AOI has risen only marginally. However, notice that the uptrends and downtrends in the two charts occur over roughly the same time spans.

The various American equity indices like the DJIA, S&P 500 and VLI move in unison over a period of time. They do not necessarily all rise and fall together on a day-by-day basis, as they cover different stocks and some are weighted while others are not.

Using a price database and computer it is easy to check the correlation between the indices. For each index we take weekly data and determine whether the week has been up or down. We then match this with a second index and the possible conditions are:

• Both indices up.

- Both indices down.

- One up and one down.

Table 12.1 lists the results for pairs of indices over either about eight years (430 weeks) or 5.5 years (288 weeks) to March 1998. The term "correlation" has a particular statistical meaning, so the term "tracking" is used here to describe the condition where both indices move in the same direction.

TABLE 12.1   Tracking Between Pairs of Indices

	DJAI/VLI	DJAI/AOI	VLI/AOI	AOI/AII	DJAI/AII
Both up	153	164	121	207	170
Both down	81	110	73	176	107
Up and down	54	156	94	47	153
Total weeks	288	430	288	430	430
% together	81	64	67	89	64

It is seen that the two Australian indices AOI and AII have a high tracking of 89%, and also the two American indices DJIA and VLI with 81%. The various pairings between the American and Australian indices result in trackings in the mid-60s.

Chapter 11 showed that the Four Percent Model works well on the VLI, but a Percent Model does not work particularly well on the AOI due to more frequent whipsaws in the Australian market.

It is of interest to take the signals from the VLI Four Percent Model and apply them to the AOI. We will not use a value of 4%, but rather 3.5% as this value gives slightly better results on the more recent VLI data. Further, this is the value used in optimising the Percent Model on the AOI, so gives a direct comparison between the two sets of signals.

Table 12.2 opposite lists the trades where the signal dates and leg directions are taken from the VLI 3.5 Percent Model, and applied to the AOI. The time span covered is 5.5 years from November 1992 to March 1998. Figure 12.1 on page 68 shows a weekly chart of the AOI marked up with these signals.

TABLE 12.2 Results For Weekly All Ordinaries Index Using Signals From VLI 3.5 Percent Model

Leg	Dir.	Signal Date	AOI Value	Rev. to Rev.	Rev. to Peak	Rev. to Rev. %
1	UP	30/10/92	1425			
		1/4/94	2053	628	925	43.9
2	DO	1/4/94	2053			
		12/8/94	2052	1	107	0
3	UP	12/8/94	2052			
		7/10/94	1967	-85	72	-4.1
4	DO	7/10/94	1967			
		30/12/94	1912	55	153	2.8
5	UP	30/12/94	1912			
		27/10/95	2067	155	260	8.1
6	DO	27/10/95	2067			
		1/12/95	2163	-96	12	-4.6
7	UP	1/12/95	2163			
		5/7/96	2231	68	173	3.1
8	DO	5/7/96	2231			
		9/8/96	2221	10	140	0
9	UP	9/8/96	2221			
		28/3/97	2422	201	287	9.0
10	DO	28/3/97	2422			
		2/5/97	2491	-69	81	-2.8
11	UP	2/5/97	2491			
		31/10/97	2464	-27	306	-1.1
12	DO	31/10/97	2464			
		30/1/98	2656	-192	33	-7.8
13	UP	30/1/98	2656			
		20/3/98	2744	88	88	3.3
	still open on 31/3/98					

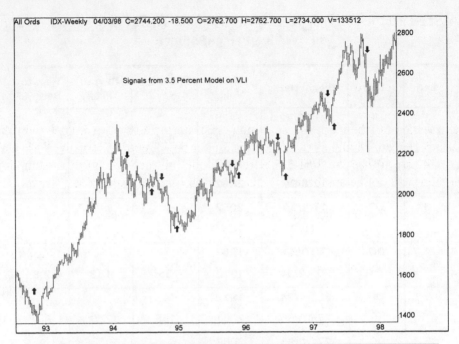

All Ords   IDX-Weekly   04/03/98 C=2744.200 -18.500 O=2762.700 H=2762.700 L=2734.000 V=133512

Signals from 3.5 Percent Model on VLI

FIGURE 12.1   Weekly All Ordinaries Index With VLI 3.5 Percent Model Signals

Table 12.2 shows there are 13 trades. If we measure the profits from AOI values at the signal dates (column 5, "Rev. to Rev."), then eight legs give a profit (62% correct), with a net profit of 737 points. Column 6, "Rev. to Peak", lists the maximum profit in each leg, and it is worth noting that each leg gives a profit. (Remember that the signals are taken from the VLI 3.5 Percent Model.)

The last column in Table 12.2 is the Rev. to Rev. profit expressed as a percentage of the opening price.

Trades 11 and 12 need some comment as they straddle the mini-crash of October 1997. The American market fell sharply on Monday 27 October, recovered the following day and in the next few months made new highs. Most of the trend-following systems were short on Friday 24 October, but surprisingly the VLI 3.5 Percent Model was not, but did go short on Friday 31 October. Checking the VLI weekly close values we find that on Friday 24 October the VLI had retraced only 2.7% from its peak, whereas the AOI had retraced 7.7% from its peak (see Appendices B and C).

By comparison, over the same 5.5 year time span the 3.5 Percent Model on the AOI gives 21 trades of which 48% give a profit, for a net profit of 1033 points.

WHERE TO NOW?

The question is when will the next mini-crash occur, and when it does, will the VLI 3.5 Percent Model already be signalling a downtrend? Alternatively, it may be quite safe to use the VLI 3.5 Percent Model on the AOI on the assumption that there will not be another stock market crash (mini or major) for 10 years.

Readers can ponder the usefulness of the VLI 3.5 Percent Model to the Australian markets. One application could be to use it as a filter with other systems like weekly MACD or the AOI 3.5 Percent Model, and take only those trades which are confirmed by the direction of the VLI 3.5 Percent Model.

Alternatively, column 6 ("Rev. to Peak") in Table 12.2 shows that every leg gives a potential profit. Thus, some form of percentage profit trailing stop may be able to capture worthwhile profits from these legs.

Chapter 13

COPPOCK INDICATOR

THIS INDICATOR WAS first published in 1962 by Edwin Coppock, and his only claim for it was as a reliable tool in selecting the low risk long-term buy points on the DJIA. It does in fact work well on the DJIA and picks about three uptrends a decade (see Steve Leuthold, Colin Nicholson).

Coppock pointed out that the indicator gives no information on when to sell, nor was it intended for short time span trading signals. However, over the years the Coppock has become a popular complete indicator, with its use extended to indices other than the DJIA, and giving both up and down signals on shorter time scales.

The Coppock indicator is essentially the sum of the 11-month momentum plus the 14-month momentum, with some smoothing added. The indicator gives a buy signal at a time of low risk, just after the start of an upward move in the market.

There are four steps involved in calculating the Coppock indicator:

1. Calculate the percentage change in value from 14 months ago.

2. Calculate the percentage change in value from 11 months ago.

3. Add item 1 and item 2.

4. The indicator is the 10-month weighted average of item 3.

The maths for the indicator is given in Appendix A.

The Coppock indicator is normally plotted as a histogram which moves above and below zero. An uptrend signal is given when the indicator is below zero and turns upward.

The central trace of Figure 13.1 shows the monthly AOI with the Coppock indicator displayed as a histogram under the index. The five up signals over the past 15 years are indicated by the arrows on the price plot ('PM' stands for 'Poor Man's Coppock Indicator' – see below), and in each case the AOI rose after the signal was given. The Coppock signal given in 1988 was followed by about nine months of sideways movement in the AOI before rising marginally. It is sometimes argued that the dramatic fall in the market in October 1987 would skew technical indicators, thus the next signal given should be treated with great caution.

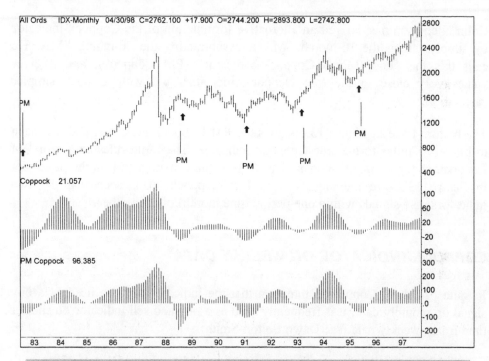

FIGURE 13.1 Monthly All Ordinaries Index With Coppock Indicators

Why No Coppock Down Signals?

Inspection of the Coppock indicator in the central trace of Figure 13.1 shows that each time the indicator falls below zero, it forms a single well-defined trough before moving back into positive territory. The indicator trough coincides with the start of an AOI uptrend, thus giving a reliable signal of this new uptrend.

When the AOI moves in long uptrends, as from 1983 to 1987, and from 1995 to 1998, the Coppock indicator produces multiple peaks without moving into negative territory. In these cases, the indicator peaks coincide with a minor downtrend in the index. However, in 1992 and 1994 the indicator produced single peaks, which did coincide with the start of sustained downtrends in the AOI.

Thus Coppock indicator peaks are a much more hit and miss affair in signalling downtrends, than are the reliable uptrend signals.

POOR MAN'S COPPOCK INDICATOR

Colin Nicholson has derived an alternative formulation of the Coppock indicator by simply taking the 10-month SMA and subtracting the 20-month SMA. He calls this the "Poor Man's Coppock indicator" (PM Coppock), and it gives values very close to the true Coppock indicator, but with a much simpler calculation.

The bottom trace in Figure 13.1 shows the PM Coppock indicator, and it is seen to be very similar to the true Coppock indicator. The same rules apply for PM Coppock as for normal Coppock. The vertical lines marked PM on the price plot in Figure 13.1 are the signals from PM Coppock. It is seen that the two indicators give signals within one period (one month) of each other.

COPPOCK INDICATOR ON WEEKLY DATA

In spite of Edwin Coppock's intention that the indicator only be used as a buy signal on monthly data, it is frequently used as a buy and sell indicator on shorter time frame weekly data (see Dawn Bolton-Smith).

Figure 13.2 opposite shows a five-year segment of weekly AOI data along with the Coppock and PM Coppock indicators, using the same parameter values as for the monthly data i.e. 11,14,10 for the Coppock indicator and 10,20 for the PM Coppock. Figures 13.1 and 13.2 both show that the Coppock indicators make single troughs below the zero line, but when they move above zero, they sometimes makes multiple peaks before returning to negative territory (see regions A, B, C in Figure 13.2).

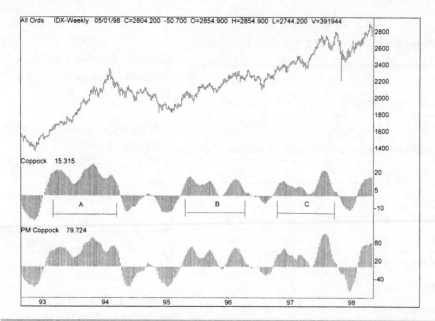

FIGURE 13.2   Weekly All Ordinaries Index With Coppock Indicators

We recall that the monthly Coppock indicator is only used to give up signals, and has the simple logic:

- An uptrend signal is given when the indicator is below zero and turns upward.

In the case of the weekly data we can either maintain this logic, or look for ways of generating both up and down signals.

Both Figures 13.1 and 13.2 show that the Coppock indicator is very good at picking uptrends, as the troughs of the indicator below the zero line coincide very closely with the start of fresh uptrends in the index. Region A in Figure 13.2 (and to a lesser extent regions B, C) shows that the weekly Coppock can exhibit multiple peaks and troughs above the zero line during the course of a sustained rise in the index. Consequently, any logic chosen to indicate the start of an index downtrend cannot depend solely on the Coppock indicator turning down from peak territory.

One simple set of logic rules for the weekly Coppock indicator is:

- A buy signal is given when the indicator crosses upwards through zero.

- A sell signal is given when the indicator crosses downwards through zero.

TABLE 13.1   Results For Weekly All Ordinaries Index With Coppock Indicator

	Coppock
Open first trade	21/9/90
Opening index value	1428
Close last trade	6/2/98
Closing index value	2656
Net profit	899
Gross profit	1376
Gross loss	-477
Number of trades	17
% profitable	53
Average profit trade	153
Average losing trade	-60
Ratio avg. profit/avg. loss	2.5
Max. consecutive profits	3
Max. consecutive losses	3
Average weeks in profits	35
Average weeks in losses	9

Using this logic to analyse the 7.5 year weekly AOI data of Chapter 6, the results for the Coppock indicator are given in Table 13.1.

Comparing these weekly Coppock results with the weekly MACD benchmark results in Chapter 6, we see that the Coppock net profit is a little less than the 1014 points obtained from the MACD, but the number of trades has fallen from 23 to 17.

IMPROVING THE WEEKLY COPPOCK INDICATOR

Inspection of Figure 13.2 shows that the simple zero crossing logic used above with the weekly data has its good features, but also some bad ones.

The good feature is that Coppock gets us into, and holds us in, the long uptrends such as those occurring at regions A, B and C discussed above.

The bad feature is that the zero crossing is always late in giving the entry and exit signals. The timing of the indicator peaks and troughs are better matched to the changes in trend in the index.

There are various ways that the weekly Coppock indicator might be improved, and the goals are:

• To produce a histogram having single peaks and troughs above and below zero, with these peaks and troughs coinciding with the changes in the index trends.

• Alternatively, to produce a histogram having zero crossings close to the changes in the index trends.

Some suggestions to achieve the goals are as follows:

1. Experiment with values other than 11-period and 14-period momentum in the Coppock formulation. Longer periods are likely to be better for weekly data.

2. Consider ways of defining the major peaks and troughs, while avoiding any spurious ones.

3. There are a number of techniques to pick peaks and troughs, viz.:

   a. Apply a 3-week or 4-week SMA to the indicator. The indicator peaks and troughs are defined by the indicator crossing below or above the SMA respectively.

   b. Extend the Coppock logic to use two, or maybe three, consecutive up values to define a valid trough, and for weekly data the indicator may be either below or above the zero line. Similarly, use two, or maybe three, consecutive down values to define a valid peak, and for weekly data the indicator may be either above or below the zero line.

   c. For the mathematically minded, calculate the gradient of the indicator. The gradient value crosses zero from above at the peak, and crosses zero from below at the trough, thereby giving a clear signal that a peak or trough has occurred.

Readers with a database and charting software may like to experiment with the maths of the Coppock indicator along the above lines. I suspect that playing with Coppock indicators needs be done on the true Coppock formulation, not the simpler PM Coppock. The reason for this is that the starting point for the Coppock indicator is two momentum calculations, and the momentum indicator can produce a leading signal (see LeBeau and Lucas). Conversely, the starting point for the PM Coppock is two SMA calculations, and the SMA is definitely a lagging indicator. Remember, the goal is to find an indicator which give peaks and troughs (or zero crossings) coincident with the index peaks and troughs, not lagging several weeks behind them.

WEEKLY COPPOCK INDICATOR WITH DIFFERENT PARAMETERS

Considering the first suggestion above, we could structure the weekly Coppock indicator to analyse the same amount of data as does the monthly indicator. Thus the 11-month, 14-month and 10-month parameters are replaced by 44-week, 56-week and 40-week values respectively. The Coppock indicators with these sets of parameters are designated as Coppock 11,14,10 and Coppock 44,56,40 respectively. Figure 13.3 shows a 10-year plot of the weekly AOI along with these two indicators.

Comparison of the weekly Coppock 44,56,40 bottom trace in Figure 13.3 with the monthly Coppock central trace in Figure 13.1, shows the peaks, troughs and zero crossings occur at substantially the same times. Unfortunately, but understandably, the weekly Coppock 44,56,40 displays the same multiple peaks above zero as does the monthly Coppock indicator.

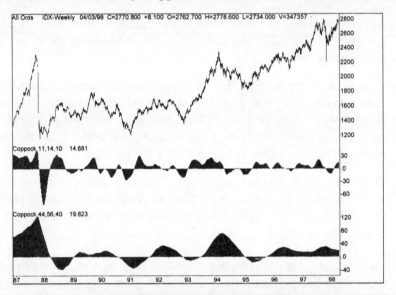

FIGURE 13.3   Weekly All Ordinaries Index With Coppock 11,14,10 And Coppock 44,56,40 Indicators

TRENDEX CONFIDENCE INDICATOR

As a matter of interest, the finance newsletter *Trendex* uses a proprietary indicator which it calls the Confidence Index, to pick the important trends in the market. The Confidence Index usually produces single peaks and troughs on the ASX weekly indices.

A new uptrend is signalled when the Confidence Index is below zero and turns up. The uptrend is confirmed when the Confidence Index crosses above zero. Similarly, a new downtrend is signalled when the Confidence Index is above zero and turns down. The downtrend is confirmed when the Confidence Index crosses below zero.

The Confidence Index was developed by Dr Garretty, the founder of Trendex in Australia, and is based on the Coppock indicator, but not identical to it.

Chapter 14

ADVANCE/DECLINE LINE

THE ADVANCE/DECLINE (A/D) line is called a breadth of market indicator, and is an alternative and important method for showing strength and weakness in the overall market. The A/D line is applied to a group of stocks, so is ideal for tracking the various indices.

As mentioned in Chapter 2, the AOI at February 1998 comprised some 299 of the larger capitalisation stocks drawn from all sectors of the market. The total number of stocks listed on the ASX is around 1200.

To calculate a daily A/D line for the AOI, each day the number of falling stocks in the overall market is deducted from the number of rising stocks in the overall market, and the resulting value is added to yesterday's A/D value, thus giving a cumulative tally. Over a period of time the A/D line builds up a valuable picture of the buying and selling pressure in the overall market – whereas the index itself is a measure of the value of the leaders. There can be subtle differences between the shape of the index and the A/D line, which offer clues as to the future direction of the index. For example, one of the conditions we are looking for with the A/D line is those times when the junior stocks diverge from the leaders.

The A/D line is particularly good in warning of the end of market uptrends, and is a valuable tool for technical analysts. However, the mechanics of calculating the A/D line for the various indices need be fully understood, and care must be taken in choosing the sources of data used for this purpose.

One feature of the A/D line is that it is unweighted, because if NAB rises it increases the A/D tally by 1 for the day, while if some smaller stock falls it decreases the tally by 1. The two moves cancel one another to give a net contribution of 0 to the A/D line for that day.

DAILY AND WEEKLY DATA

The A/D line can be calculated for daily, weekly or monthly data, but all three are calculated differently. Consider a stock with the following daily close prices:

Fri	Mon	Tues	Wed	Thur	Fri
100	101	103	106	105	105

For a daily A/D line the stock contributions are 1, 1, 1, -1, 0 giving a net +2 over the five days from Monday to Friday. For a weekly A/D line the stock contribution from Friday to Friday is +1.

Suppose we calculate our own A/D line data and enter it into a spreadsheet, to be subsequently read by charting software and displayed as a chart. Some charting packages allow daily stock price data to be converted and displayed as weekly data by one or two keystokes. If we attempt this with daily A/D line data the subsequent train of weekly numbers is meaningless, for the reasons discussed above.

RULES FOR TRADING THE A/D LINE

The A/D line is read in conjunction with the parent index, and the two charts should be plotted together on the same page with the same time scale, as shown in Figures 14.1(a) and 14.1(b) for the daily AOI. (See page 80.)

The A/D line measures the breadth of market, which is what the market as a whole is doing. The index, however, measures only what the leaders are doing.

In a healthy bull market, the broad market is advancing along with the leaders. As the bull trend ends investors tend to quit their junior stocks, while holding onto quality i.e. the index stocks. A divergence at this time tells us that the rats and mice are deserting the ship. Consequently, the A/D line will normally turn down before the index does (see particularly rule 4 below).

At the bottom of a bear market the junior stocks still keep going down even after the leaders start to advance. This is caused by the "flight to quality", and also the canny investors buying into stocks which will lead the market up. Thus at market bottoms the daily A/D line does not normally move up before the index does, so gives no indication of the impending market upturn.

The rules for reading the A/D line with the index are (see Merril Armstrong, William Jiler):

Togetherness

1. When the A/D line and the index are both moving in the same direction, then the index trend is likely to continue.

Disparity

2. When the index falls while its A/D line is rising, the index will turn up.

3. When the index rises while its A/D line is falling, the index will turn down.

4. When the index approaches a previous top and the A/D line is below its value at that previous top, the index will turn down. If the A/D line is above its value at the previous top, new index highs are likely.

5. When the index approaches a previous low and the A/D line is above its value at the previous low, the index will turn up. If the A/D line is below its value at the previous low, new index lows are likely.

These rules are not infallible, but are helpful in reading the A/D line in conjunction with index plots.

It should be stressed that the A/D line *does not give a timing signal*, but can be used to give advance warning of a change in the index trend.

The A/D line can also be analysed with normal charting procedures. For example, with the A/D line drawn on a linear plot, trend lines can be drawn and a reversal signal for the index is given when a trend line on the A/D chart is penetrated (see Chapters 18, 19 and Dawn Bolton-Smith).

EXAMPLE OF DIVERGENCE AT MARKET TOPS

Figures 14.1(a) and 14.1(b) for the daily AOI and daily A/D line (both overleaf) show a classic example of divergence at market tops. In Figure 14.1(a) the AOI peak B is higher than peak A, while peak C is higher than peak B. However, turning to the daily A/D line plot in Figure 14.1(b), we see that point Y is below point X, which is a divergence and indication of a coming downturn in the AOI. Further, point Z is below point Y, showing a second even greater divergence, and reinforcing the inevitability of a coming downturn. History (and Figure 14.1(a)), shows there were a few days to get positioned for the 500-point fall during October 1997.

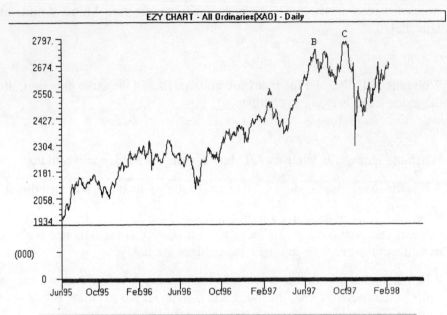

FIGURE 14.1(a)   Daily All Ordinaries Index Over 2.5 Years

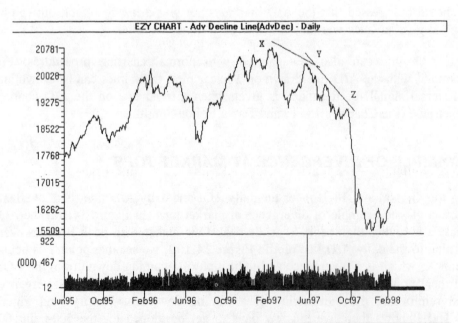

FIGURE 14.1(b)   Daily All Ordinaries Index A/D Line Over 2.5 Years

CALCULATING THE A/D LINE

It is possible to calculate A/D data by hand using data published daily in the *Australian Financial Review* (*AFR*). Each day stock advances and declines are shown in the section on Sharemarket Indices in the form of the table listed below:

National Exchange	Rises	Falls	Steady	TOTAL
Industrial				
Mining				
Oil				
TOTAL				

Rather than use hand calculation, it is easier to use a data supplier and charting software. Users should check that the data provided is accurate, and do this by checking against the figures in the *AFR* from time to time. If the figures do not agree, then contact the data provider to find the cause of the discrepancy. Further, some data suppliers provide A/D line data on indices like the 50 Leaders. This can be misleading, as the whole rationale behind the A/D line is comparing movements in an index with the total stocks in that sector of the market.

The software package Ezy Charts available from E.I.S. Production calculates the A/D line for any of the individual ASX indices. It can also be made to calculate the A/D lines for the indices like the AOI which contain stocks covering various market sectors. The steps involved in calculating the AOI daily A/D line are given in Appendix D.

Some analysts collect data from the *AFR* to calculate four A/D lines as:

1. All industrial stocks, which is compared with the All Industrials Index.

2. All mining stocks, which is compared with the All Mining Index.

3. Oil (and gas) stocks, which is compared with the Energy Index.

4. A total of the above three A/D values, which represents all ASX stocks, which is then compared with the AOI.

Alternatively, the data is collected for the three major sectors, but only the total A/D values are calculated and compared against the AOI. It would also be possible to plot a total of the mining and oil (and gas) A/D values, to compare against the All Resources Index.

ALTERNATIVE PRESENTATIONS OF A/D DATA

Zweig uses an alternative formulation of the numbers of rising and falling stocks by taking their ratio, rather than the cumulative sum, which he calls the Advance/Decline Ratio.

The A/D Ratio is the number of rising stocks divided by the number of falling stocks for the day, with steady stocks being ignored. He then takes the 10-day moving average of this ratio, and has found that when it exceeds 2:1 it is a sign that the market's upward momentum is strong.

He calculates the A/D Ratio using the stocks traded on the NYSE, and found that from 1953 to 1985 there were only eight instances of this A/D Ratio average exceeding 2:1. There were also one or two instances when a second signal was given within a couple of months of the first signal, so was part of the same upward drive. In each of the eight cases the market value as measured by the S&P 500 index was 10% higher six months after the A/D Ratio signal, and in two cases was more than 25% higher.

From the small number of signals it is apparent that this is not a trading signal, but one to pay attention to when it occurs, and then decide on how to participate in the anticipated strong upward move in the market.

Some readers may get A/D cumulative data from their data suppliers. It is not possible to convert this data to the A/D Ratio, as to calculate the ratio it is necessary to have the individual number of daily rises and falls. If readers have daily data in spreadsheet form, it is possible to calculate the A/D Ratio.

STUDY THE A/D LINE

Technical analysts usually have a handful of favourite technical indicators and charting techniques which they use to monitor the market, and so determine changes in trends. The A/D line is considered the best of the breadth of market indicators. It is not to be used in isolation, but does offer advance warning of changes in trends.

It is worthwhile spending time to understand the A/D line and its rules, and applying it to a number of indices to see it in action. This in turn will involve getting historic A/D data, probably from one of the data suppliers discussed in Chapter 31.

It is essential that the calculated or provided A/D data be checked against the values listed in the *AFR* (or other daily newspapers), which are the official values from the ASX. Only when the two sets of A/D values agree can the rules listed on page 79 be used.

Alternatively, A/D data on the daily AOI may be available from ATAA members who have collected it over the years.

Some analysts use the monthly Coppock indicator to pick the start of market uptrends, and the daily A/D line divergence to warn of an end to the trend. This gives the "big picture" on the market. Knowing that the overall market trend is up or down can be a great help in the way we go about our investing or trading.

Chapter 15

POINT AND FIGURE CHARTING

TO DATE WE have shown charts of the various indices as either line charts or bar charts. A weekly line chart draws a line through the weekly close prices. Alternatively, a weekly bar chart draws a vertical bar for each week, with the upper and lower values of the bar corresponding to the weekly high and low values respectively. The close price for the week is displayed as a short horizontal line attached to the vertical bar, and pointing to the right (see Figure 8.2).

A point and figure (P&F) chart is a series of columns of X and O symbols on a sheet of squared paper, with the X symbols indicating rising prices and the O symbols representing falling prices. The main feature to note about the P&F chart is that it takes no account of time, as price is the only parameter in the chart.

P&F charts are used to give buy and sell signals, and also price targets which are likely to be achieved in the subsequent moves. Analysts often keep both bar charts and P&F charts, as together they build up a more complete picture of the past behaviour of a stock or index, and likely future moves.

CONSTRUCTING A P&F CHART

The basic rules for constructing a P&F chart are:

1. Mark a series of Xs in the column while the price is rising.

2. Mark a series of Os in the column while the price is falling.

3. There must be at least *two* entries in each completed column.

Rule 3 means that if the value reverses after a single entry in a column, then we add entries in this same column until the next reversal moves us to a fresh column. Consequently a column can contain a series of Xs sitting on a O, or a series of Os underneath a X. (One way of visualising this is that we move to a new column when the box we want to occupy is already taken.)

Suppose we wish to draw a P&F chart of the AOI. The first thing to decide is the "box size". The box size is the number of points the index must move for a new X or O to be added to the chart. The movements charted are not close of day, or close of week, but are intra-day values.

Suppose we select a box size of 5 points and the AOI intra-day variations over a series of days are:

Day 1	2550, 2561, 2559
Day 2	2562, 2554, 2566, 2564
Day 3	2574
Day 4	2559, 2576

The corresponding P&F chart is shown in Figure 15.1. We start by drawing three Xs corresponding to the move from 2550 to 2561. The move down to 2559 followed by the rise to 2562 are ignored, as they do not fill a whole box. On day 2 the fall to 2554 results in a single O in the next column, but the reversal to 2566 requires two Xs being drawn above the O in column 2. On day 3 the value continues up to 2574 so another X is added in the same column. Then on day 4 the value drops to 2559 so a fresh column is entered with two Os. The final value of 2576 opens a new column with three Os.

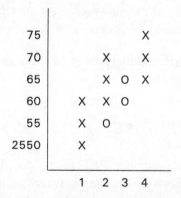

FIGURE 15.1 Construction of a Point and Figure Chart

It is apparent that the value chosen for the box size will influence the amount of detail presented in the chart. The above example using a 5 point box size results in four columns on a P&F chart. If the box size is 1 point, many more columns would be produced using the same set of data. Thus the box size acts as a filter on the data variations, and eliminates some of the unwanted noise.

Initially P&F charts were constructed by hand, which is a somewhat tedious exercise. With the advent of the personal computer and charting software, P&F charts can be drawn very quickly and box sizes changed by a few key strokes.

The box size needs be related to the stock price (or index value). There are no hard and fast rules as larger box size means more filtering of the unwanted noise, but at the expense of losing useful detail within the P&F chart. Some analysts adopt the following relationship:

Stock Price	Box Size
11 to 30	1
31 to 60	2
61 to 100	5

Using charting software, a range of box sizes can be tried in order to give satisfactory chart detail for analysis.

THREE POINT REVERSAL CHARTS

An extension of the basic P&F chart is the three point reversal chart (or 3-box reversal). In this case the index value must reverse direction by at least three box values for a new column to be drawn on the chart, and the column will have a minimum of three entries. In the above example, the index must reverse at least 15 points for a new column to be drawn.

Three point reversal charts eliminate more of the noise on the data, leaving the bare bones of the price action.

P&F CHARTING SOFTWARE

The above discussion showed that P&F charts are draw using intra-day data. When P&F charts are drawn by charting software, some assumptions have to be made, because the data available is usually daily open, high, low and close values. No information is available on intra-day moves. Further, it is not apparent whether the day's high occurred before the day's low, or vice versa.

Different charting packages use different algorithms to calculate the P&F charts. P&F programs allow user selection of the box size and the number of box reversals. Unfortunately, some of these algorithms have errors. One error in some software is that rule 3 listed above is not adhered to, and the software incorrectly produces a chart which can have a single X or O in a column, when a 1-box reversal is chosen. If our charting software displays this fault, it can be overcome by drawing 2-box reversal charts, which are then correct.

P&F CHART FORMATIONS

Much of the value of the P&F chart lies in the patterns which are produced, and a subsequent breakout from these patterns. Some of the important patterns are:

- Congestion areas

- Channels

- Triangles

- Flags, pennants and wedges

- Fulcrum

- Head and shoulders

- The V

- Saucers.

Examples of some of these patterns are given below and in subsequent chapters. An excellent treatment of P&F charts is found in Armstrong and also in Wheelan, with a shorter coverage in Meani.

P&F CHARTS FOR ALL ORDINARIES INDEX

When using computer software to draw P&F charts the appropriate box size can be determined by trial and error. The object is to produce a chart which reflects the major moves in the indices but eliminates some of the noise. A typical box size is about 1% or 2% of the index value. Similarly, it is worthwhile experimenting with different numbers of box reversals to filter out the noise.

Figure 15.2 opposite shows the P&F chart for AOI using a 20 point box size and 3-box reversal. The horizontal axis shows time graduations, but these are only approximate. Figure 15.2 and the weekly AOI of Figure 13.1 cover the same time frame, but notice that the dates for the P&F peaks and troughs do not correspond very closely to the true index peaks and troughs. (This is a program limitation and does not affect the accuracy of the P&F chart.)

The P&F chart clearly shows the major peaks and troughs A,B,C,D,E,F,G,H,I,J. In terms of Dow Theory, the sequence C,D,E,F,G,H is an uptrend with higher highs and higher lows. The low I is below the previous low G, so introduces a note of caution. However, in mid-April 1998 the AOI reached a new high J above the previous high H, thereby reinstating the uptrend (though maybe only temporarily).

Figure 15.3 opposite shows the P&F chart for the AOI using a 10 point box size with a 2-box reversal. The chart covers the segment F,G,H,I,J from Figure 15.2, but now shows finer detail. This finer P&F chart can be used to determine breakouts from patterns. BO1 is an example of a breakout from a channel, BO2 is a breakout from a consolidation region and BO3 is a breakout from an ascending triangle.

From time to time P&F charts give classic breakout signals. Technical analysts may act on these signals, or alternatively use them to confirm signals from other indicators like the MACD, etc.

P&F CHART PRESENTATION

When P&F charts are drawn by hand squared paper is used, so each X or O sits in its own little square box. When the charts are drawn by computer, the user selects the length of time segment to analyse, and the software automatically scales the vertical axis to accommodate the minimum and maximum index levels over that time. The net result is that the computer-drawn P&F chart may have to generate rectangles rather than squares to hold the X and O symbols. Consequently, the P&F charts may look a bit clumsy sometimes, but they still show the important P&F features.

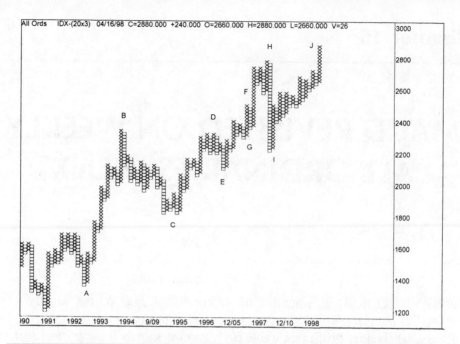

FIGURE 15.2   Coarse Point and Figure Chart For All Ordinaries Index

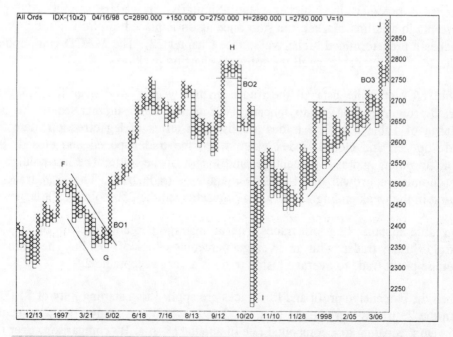

FIGURE 15.3   Fine Point and Figure Chart For All Ordinaries Index

Chapter 16

MACD REVISITED ON WEEKLY ALL ORDINARIES INDEX

WE HAVE LOOKED at a number of technical indicators on the weekly AOI. The MACD indicator with 250 point profit target stops is the preferred method as it gives a satisfactory profit (see Table 6.1), and the signals for entry and exit are clear and unambiguous. Further, this type of stop order is accepted by any stockbroker, as in a rising market the stop is placed to quit when the price reaches a predetermined higher value. Similarly, if we are trading AOI put warrants in a falling market, the stop once again is placed to quit when the price reaches a predetermined higher value (see Chapter 22). The MACD is a popular indicator so is available on all the software charting packages.

Table 16.1 opposite lists all the trades on the weekly AOI over the 7.5 year period from August 1990 to January 1998 which were summarised in the last column of Table 6.1. The trades are listed in terms of leg direction, date the trade opened and closed, index value when the trade opened and closed, leg profit in points and as a percentage, and length of the trade. The last column is the cumulative growth of $1,000 on a trade-by-trade basis. The final trade is closed in the week ending 31/10/97 having achieved the 250 point profit target.

The table contains 12 profit trades with an average percentage profit of 10.7%, and 11 losing trades with an average percentage loss of -3.7%. The ratio of average profit trade to average losing trade is a very acceptable 2.9.

When the percentage profit and loss trades are applied to a starting kitty of $1,000, then the 23 trades increase the kitty to $2,192, which is a gain of 120% over the 7.5 years, equating to a compound rate of about 11% p.a. By comparison, over the 7.5 years the AOI moves from 1470 to 2416 for a gain of 64%.

TABLE 16.1   Profit on Weekly All Ordinaries Index With MACD And 250 Point Profit Target Stop

No.	Leg Direction	Date	AOI Value	Profit (Points)	%	Weeks	$1,000 Growth
1	Down	24/8/90	1469.6				
		18/1/91	1219.6	250.0	17.0	21	1,170
2	Up	1/2/91	1302.5				
		3/5/91	1552.5	250.0	19.2	13	1,395
3	Down	23/8/91	1540.8				
		25/10/91	1641.6	-100.8	-6.5	9	1,304
4	Up	25/10/91	1641.6				
		6/12/91	1583.8	-57.8	-3.5	6	1,258
5	Down	6/12/91	1583.8				
		1/5/92	1665.2	-81.4	-5.1	21	1,194
6	Up	1/5/92	1665.2				
		10/7/92	1644.4	-20.8	-1.2	10	1,180
7	Down	10/7/92	1644.4				
		13/11/92	1394.4	250.0	15.2	18	1,359
8	Up	11/12/92	1500.7				
		28/5/93	1750.7	250.0	16.7	24	1,586
9	Down	25/6/93	1700.4				
		2/7/93	1768.9	-68.5	-4.0	1	1,523
10	Up	2/7/93	1768.9				
		8/10/93	2018.9	250.0	14.1	14	1,738
11	Down	26/11/93	2043.1				
		7/1/94	2186.0	-142.9	-7.0	6	1,616

No.	Leg Direction	Date	AOI Value	Profit Points	%	Weeks	$1,000 Growth
12	Up	7/1/94	2186.0				
		25/2/94	2148.8	-37.2	-1.7	7	1,589
13	Down	25/2/94	2148.8				
		12/8/94	2051.9	96.9	4.5	24	1,661
14	Up	12/8/94	2051.9				
		30/9/94	2028.7	-23.2	-1.1	7	1,643
15	Down	30/9/94	2028.7				
		24/2/95	1911.1	117.6	5.8	21	1,738
16	Up	24/2/95	1911.1				
		15/9/95	2161.1	250.0	13.1	29	1,966
17	Down	6/10/95	2098.2				
		8/12/95	2186.1	-87.9	-4.2	9	1,883
18	Up	8/12/95	2186.1				
		15/3/96	2234.8	48.7	2.2	14	1,924
19	Down	15/3/96	2234.8				
		23/8/96	2292.9	-58.1	-2.6	23	1,874
20	Up	23/8/96	2292.9				
		14/3/97	2423.2	130.3	5.7	29	1,981
21	Down	14/3/97	2423.2				
		9/5/97	2526.0	-102.8	-4.2	8	1,898
22	Up	9/5/97	2526.0				
		15/8/97	2666.2	140.2	5.6	14	2,004
23	Down	15/8/97	2666.2				
		31/10/97	2416.2	250.0*	9.4	11	2,192

*Profit target stop triggered by intra-week low

92

Chapter 22 shows the gearing on the AOI warrants to be about three times. Thus the percentage returns on the warrants using the above MACD system on the historic data give theoretical profits around 33% p.a. In practice the results will be less, due to slippage and brokerage charges.

However, if the AOI follows similar trending patterns in the future as in the past, then trading the AOI warrants using the MACD system with profit target stops should be a profitable exercise.

BACK-TESTING THE SECOND SEGMENT OF DATA

In Chapter 3 the concept of back-testing was discussed, whereby a technical indicator is applied to historic data partitioned into several time segments. If the indicator works well over a number of time segments, we have added confidence that it will continue to work well in the future.

We now turn our attention to analysing the weekly AOI with the preferred MACD indicator on an earlier segment of data spanning six years from August 1984 to August 1990 (see Figure 3.1). This data is of considerable interest as it spans the October 1987 crash. Table 16.2 overleaf shows the results for MACD on this six-year segment of data. Column 2 gives the results using the basic MACD indicator with no stops.

Table 16.2 shows that during the six-year time span, the AOI moved from 712 points to 1478 points, for a net gain of 766 points. The MACD produced a net profit of 1813 points during this time, by trading both the uptrends and downtrends in the index.

Figure 16.1 on page 95 presents the six years of weekly AOI data with MACD signals displayed as up and down arrows. Also shown is the system equity trace. The trades immediately before, and immediately after, the October 1987 crash are of interest.

Figure 16.1 shows that the MACD went short on the week preceding the crash. The relevant AOI values leading up to the crash were:

Friday 16 October	Close 2144 points
Monday 19 October	Close 2065 points
Tuesday 20 October	Open 1549 points

TABLE 16.2 Results For MACD On Weekly All Ordinaries Index

	MACD	Floor 250 Point Percent 25
Open first trade	3/8/84	3/8/84
Opening index value	712	712
Close last trade	7/9/90	7/9/90
Closing index value	1478	1478
Net profit	1813	1943
Gross profit	2496	2626
Gross loss	-683	-683
Number of trades	23	23
% profitable	52	52
Average profit trade	208	218
Average losing trade	-62	-62
Ratio avg. profit/avg. loss	3.3	3.5
Max. consecutive profits	4	4
Max. consecutive losses	4	4
Average weeks in profits	21	20
Average weeks in losses	7	7

Our strategy is to do the analysis during the weekend using the weekly close data, and place orders on the following Monday morning. Thus, the weekend preceding the crash we obtained the MACD sell signal with the Friday AOI close at 2144 points. On Monday the AOI closed at 2065 points, but during the day we had ample time to close long positions and open short positions. Monday evening, Australian time, the DJIA fell out of bed, and Tuesday morning the AOI opened 500 points down at 1549 points. The horse had bolted and it was too late to shut the stable door.

Two points are worth noting. Firstly, the trend-following MACD gave a signal prior to the crash. Secondly, having established a strategy, it is essential to follow it to the letter. In this admittedly rather special case, to procrastinate just one day resulted in disaster.

A third point regarding MACD on weekly AOI, is that in the mini-crash in October 1997, the indicator was short some weeks before the one-day fall (see the last down arrow in Figure 6.1).

Inspection of the system equity trace in Figure 16.1 shows that most of the profit comes from the two trades before, and the two trades after, the October 1987 crash. For the remainder of this second data segment the AOI is trading in a trading range. As the MACD is a trend-following indicator, it is unable to extract profits from this type of price pattern.

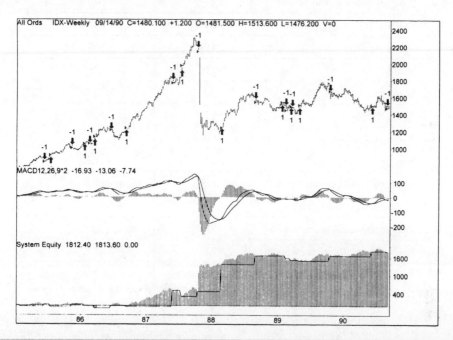

FIGURE 16.1 MACD On Weekly All Ordinaries Index Plus System Equity

Application of Stops

In Chapter 6 it was shown that a profit target stop of 250 points improved the MACD performance on the weekly AOI, for the 7.5 year segment being analysed.

Applying profit stops to the second segment of data does not produce any meaningful result. The optimum profit stop is 975 points, which captures the maximum profit from the October 1987 fall, but only increases the net profit from 1813 points to 1845 points.

Applying percentage profit trailing stops gives more realistic optimum values of 250 point floor with 25% retracement. The results for this case are shown in the last column of Table 16.2. The net profit is now 1943 points.

We conclude that the analysis of the second segment of data does nothing to detract from our selection of MACD as a preferred indicator on weekly AOI. It is comforting to know that it was short prior to the October 1987 crash.

Chapter 17

MORE ON INDICATORS

SO FAR WE have discussed various methods of technical analysis for the indices. These indicators involve some number crunching, and give a clear signal of the start and end of trends. The indicators are shown to have varying profitability on the AOI.

We now turn our attention to a number of other fiscal methods which are generally considered as reliable barometers of the overall state of the market, but do not require number crunching.

DOW THEORY

No discussion on stock market analysis is complete without some mention of the Dow Theory, named after Charles Dow. He is regarded as the father of technical analysis, and died in 1902. Over the years the theory has been refined by several practitioners, and a concise exposition is given by Martin Pring in *Technical Analysis Explained*.

Dow theory is concerned with determining the direction of the market trend, and also the US business cycle. These days the theory is applied to individual stocks and indices as well, in determining their trends.

Initially Dow confined the analysis to a basket of 12 industrial stocks and 12 railroad stocks on the New York Stock Exchange, and for each group calculated the daily average of their closing prices. The end of a market downtrend (uptrend) was signalled when both averages turned up (down). His reasoning was that business produced goods which transport carried around the country. Thus, in a bull market both sectors would be expanding, and in a bear market both sectors would be contracting. These days the DJIA and the Transportation Average are used in the analysis. Every good analyst knows not to rely on a single indicator, which may also have influenced Dow to seek confirmation of business trends with two indices.

Dow used the averages because he maintained that the averages discount everything, meaning that the average of the prices contain all the views of all the players buying and selling those stocks that day.

Dow defines an uptrend in the average as one where each new rally starts from a higher trough and produces a higher high. Similarly, downtrends in the average start from a lower peak and produce lower lows. Picking the trend reversals becomes a charting exercise, and Figure 17.1 shows two uptrends with different reversal patterns terminating at X, as the price moves below the previous trough.

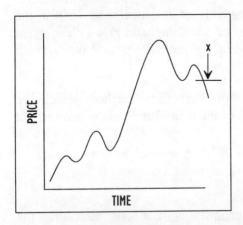 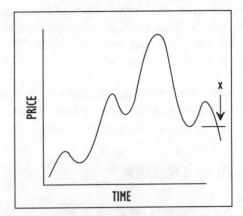

FIGURE 17.1 Examples Of Uptrend Reversals

There are a number of rules to handle the various price patterns that occur when a trend changes. Thus, some Dow followers will pick one day as the trend reversal while others may pick a different day. Remember, the object is to pick a definite reversal in the DJIA and a confirmation from the Transportation Average.

Experience shows that the Dow Theory works, and Pring shows that from 1897 to 1990 there were about 50 changes of market trend signalled, with only six being wrong. This is an impressive record, but Pring points out that the trends are subject to personal interpretation, and other analysts may come up with slightly different trend definitions. Notice also that Pring's trends have an average duration of two years, so Dow Theory is very much long term.

Applied to the Australian Market

Transposing the Dow Theory to the Australian market, either the All Industrials Index or the AOI can be used with the Australian Transport Index.

Suppose we use the All Industrials Index with the Transport Index, and rather than defining trends through inspecting charts, use the weekly MACD to define the trends in both indices.

Figures 17.2 (below) and 17.3 (overleaf) show the weekly MACD on the All Industrials Index and the Transport Index over five years. The MACD gives 20 signals on both indices, but they do not correspond in time exactly. The trading rules are:

1. An uptrend is confirmed when both the All Industrials and Transport indices are in an uptrend as defined by the MACD signals.

2. A downtrend is confirmed when both the All Industrials and Transport indices are in a downtrend as defined by the MACD signals.

One way to trade this system is to buy an Industrials Index linked fund (see Chapter 23) on the uptrend confirmation. When the downtrend is confirmed we could quit the fund and hold cash at overnight rates, and wait for the next confirmed uptrend.

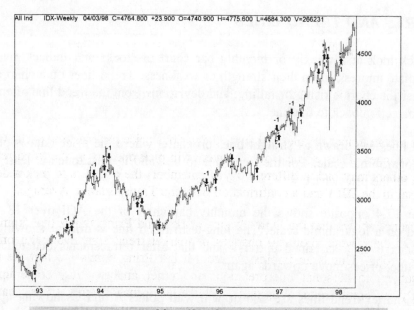

FIGURE 17.2 Weekly All Industrials Index With MACD

Applying these rules to Figures 17.2 and 17.3 show that the All Industrials Index whipsaws in October 1997 are avoided, as the Transport Index held its downtrend till early 1998.

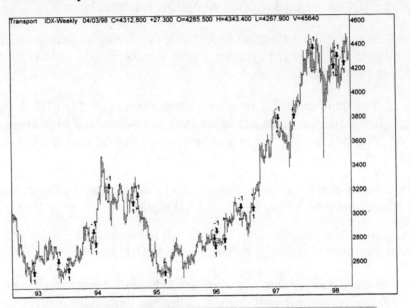

FIGURE 17.3   Weekly Transport Index With MACD

CHARTS AND TREND LINES

A quick look at a weekly or monthly bar chart of stocks and indices gives an immediate impression on their strength or weakness. Trend lines on a chart show whether the chart is rising or falling, and deviations from the trend line often lead to a correction back to the line.

Trend lines are drawn as straight lines on charts where the price data is plotted on a logarithmic scale. For the trend line to be valid it must touch at least three points on the price chart.

Figure 17.4 opposite shows the monthly bar chart of the AOI over 18 years plotted on a logarithmic scale. The long-term trend line is drawn, showing that the index is in a sustained uptrend, and that after retracements that touch the trend line, prices move upwards again.

Three shorter trend lines are also drawn, with points A and C showing upward breakouts, with B being a downward breakout.

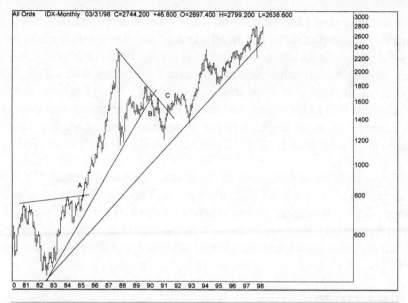

FIGURE 17.4 Monthly All Ordinaries Index With Trend Lines

Chart patterns which occur at market tops and bottoms are discussed by Regina Meani in *The Australian Investor's Guide to Charting*.

INTEREST RATES

Share prices have an inverse correlation with interest rates, because investors put their money where they can get the best overall return.

Thus the theory is that rising interest rates lead to falling share prices, and falling interest rates lead to rising share prices, all other factors being equal. The problem is that, in the real world, other factors are not equal.

The bull market in 1993 coincided with a fall in interest rates, and the bear market in 1994 happened while interest rates were rising. However, the steep fall in interest rates during 1991 to 1992 from 12% to 6% was accompanied by an uncertain market.

PRICE/EARNINGS RATIO

The Price/Earnings (P/E) Ratio for a stock is the ratio of the stock's price to the stock's annual earnings. Similarly, the Dividend Yield (DY) is the ratio of the annual dividend per share to the stock price.

The P/E is a very useful measure of the market sentiment regarding a stock. Stocks which have great expectations but small earnings can have a P/E of 30 or more, while solid but uninspiring companies may have P/Es languishing below 10. Investors looking for growth stocks usually avoid companies with a P/E above 20, while cyclical investors and contrarians search for out-of-favour stocks with abnormally low P/E ratios. However, many exciting companies do trade on high P/Es as investors are often prepared to pay a premium for the company's anticipated future growth. Thus at March 1998, News Corp has a P/E of 47, while NAB's is 14.

The ASX produces monthly figures of the average P/E and average DY ratios for stocks in the AOI and in the All Industrials Index. This is useful data and is listed in the monthly *Shares* magazine. In bull markets rising share prices lift the market P/E ratio, and abnormally high ratios are a warning sign that the end of the boom is near. Similarly, abnormally low market P/E ratios occur at the end of bear markets.

THE RULE OF 20

The Rule of 20 is a rule of thumb (see Dunstan) which is applied to both the American and Australian markets to judge the fair price of the market. The rule states:

• The market P/E plus the annual rate of inflation should add up to 20.

Figure 17.5 opposite shows the Rule of 20 from June 1960 to February 1998, published by stockbrokers HSBC James Capel in *Australian Economics, Strategy & Equity Research*, March-April 1998. The central band from 15 to 20 is deemed to be fair value, while above 20 is considered expensive with a downward correction due, and below 15 is considered cheap with an upward correction due.

The rule reflects the fact that in times of high inflation interest rates are also high, so share prices should be lower to generate equivalent yields, which in turn means lower P/E ratios. While these conditions hold the lower P/E plus the higher rate of inflation should be around 20. If share prices rise unduly along with the inflation and so exceed the Rule of 20, then a downward correction in share prices is due.

Similarly, in times of low inflation interest rates are low, so share prices should be higher to generate the equivalent yields, which in turn means higher P/E ratios. While these conditions hold the higher P/E plus the lower rate of inflation should be around 20. If share prices fall unduly with overall pessimism such that the Rule of 20 is below 15, then an upward correction in share prices is due.

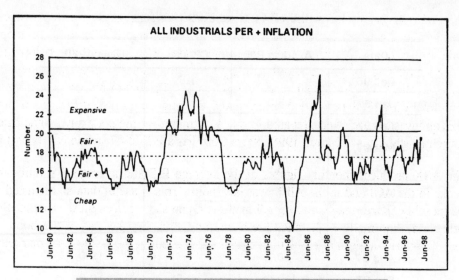

FIGURE 17.5 Plot Of Rule Of 20 Over 18 Years

A question arises as to which P/E and which annual rate of inflation to use? The ASX publishes a *Monthly ASX Index Analysis* which contains the official ASX statistics, and a number of P/E ratios are listed for All Ordinaries and All Industrials stocks. For the Rule of 20 calculations we use the "Trailing P/E for All Industrials Index Excluding Loss Makers".

Similarly, the Australian Bureau of Statistics publishes quarterly inflation rates as "Headline Inflation" and "Underlying Inflation". The Headline Inflation values (which is also called the CPI) is used in the Rule of 20 calculations for the current and the next two months.

Table 17.1 overleaf lists the Rule of 20 values on a monthly basis, as the P/E data are available monthly, even though the inflation rate is only available quarterly.

It is interesting to compare Figure 17.5 with the AOI shown in Figure 2.1. As expected, the major peaks and troughs of Figure 17.5 correspond with peaks and troughs in the AOI.

Readers are encouraged to use the Rule of 20, but care needs be taken to use consistent sources of data. The data from Table 17.1 can be extended, provided data is taken from the same sources used above. The official Trailing P/E for All Industrials Index Excluding Loss Makers is available from brokers who subscribe to *Monthly ASX Index Analysis*, while the CPI is published in the newspapers, or available from the Reserve Bank.

TABLE 17.1   Rule Of 20 Values

Date	Average P/E	CPI (%)	Rule of 20
Dec 96		1.5	
Jan 97	15.9		17.4
Feb 97	15.9		17.4
Mar 97	15.9	1.3	17.2
Apr 97	16.5		17.8
May 97	18.0		19.3
Jun 97	18.8	0.3	19.1
Jul 97	19.1		19.4
Aug 97	18.7		19.0
Sep 97	19.9	-0.3	19.6
Oct 97	17.3		17.0
Nov 97	17.9		17.6
Dec 97	18.7	-0.2	18.5
Jan 98	19.4		19.2
Feb 98	19.7		19.5

The Rule of 20 is a useful indicator of fair value. It does not give any trading signals, but it does indicate quite clearly if the overall market is overheated or unduly pessimistic. Investors need to check other indicators for signals giving the actual timing of the anticipated change in trend. However, another way for high market P/E ratios to adjust back to fair value is for earnings to increase, as from time to time in the business cycle average earnings rise.

DIVIDEND YIELD

Dividend Yield (DY) is the ratio of the annual dividend per share to the stock price. The average dividend yield for the companies in the AOI and the All Industrials Index are published each month by the ASX, and are listed in *Shares* magazine along with the average P/E ratios.

Over the past 20 years the average DY has moved around within the band bounded by 3% and 7% (though in 1974 it reached 10%). As a rule of thumb, low average DY occurs at market tops, while high average DY occurs at market bottoms.

SEASONAL FACTORS

Statistical studies on the Australian stock market show there is an annual cycle, which can be partitioned into monthly behaviour along the lines shown in Table 17.2. These monthly moves do not always occur, but the pattern happens often enough to be worthy of note.

June's weakness is caused by the Australian end of financial year with tax losses being taken, and is also the time of summer holidays in the Northern hemisphere. July is strong with portfolio buying at the start of the new financial year, as well as anticipation of half-yearly earnings reports. The Christmas rally is due to the optimism associated with a new year, and also expectations of half-yearly earnings reports.

We need to be aware of the Dec+Jan/Feb+Mar and June/July couplets and be alert to trading and investing opportunities they present.

TABLE 17.2 Seasonal Factors In The Australian Market

January	Strong month
February	Weak month
March	Down month
April	Neutral month
May	*Neutral month
June	Weakest month
July	Strongest month
August	*Neutral month
Sept, Oct, Nov	Down months
December	Start of Christmas rally

*The National Budget is brought down in one or other of these months and can move the market either way

PASCOE'S FIRST LAW OF INERTIA

Market analysis is always fickle, and even financial models linking inflation, interest rates, exchange rates, etc. to market forces and prices that worked well one year may become meaningless the next.

Michael Pascoe, Channel 9's business commentator, writing in *Your Trading Edge* sums up both technical and fundamental analysis in Pascoe's First Law of Inertia:

- "Things, systems and understandings that work well will continue to work well – until they don't."

And that is the challenge investors face. *Listen to the Market* is the title of a book on analysis by Ivan Krastins. That phrase has a ring of truth, as the market charts its own course. Usually the best we can do is move in the same direction, using trend-following techniques, some of which are discussed in this book.

Chapter 18

ANALYSIS OF WEEKLY GOLD INDEX

IN EARLIER CHAPTERS a number of indicators have been demonstrated on the AOI. In this chapter we turn out attention to the Gold Index, as this index has call warrants available for trading (see Chapter 21). A briefer analysis is presented on the Gold Index than was conducted on the AOI, as the intention is to demonstrate using a single technical indicator in conjunction with two charting techniques. The technical indicator chosen is our favourite MACD, while the two charting techniques are the A/D line and P&F charts.

The MACD gives a feel for how well the index behaves from a trending point of view, along with providing entry and exit signals. The A/D line gives warnings of trend reversals, while the P&F chart shows the breakouts from patterns, so is a complementary timing tool to the MACD.

Readers with databases and software packages may like to apply some of the other technical indicators discussed in earlier chapters to the Gold Index.

MACD

The weekly Gold Index is shown in Figure 2.4 and has sharp up and down moves, so is likely to be a good trading counter. We start by applying the weekly MACD indicator using no stops as discussed in Chapter 6, and the results are listed in column 2 of Table 18.1 opposite for the eight years from October 1989 to February 1998.

106

TABLE 18.1   Results For MACD On Weekly Gold Index

	MACD	Floor 175 Point Percent 40
Open first trade	13/10/89	13/10/89
Opening index value	1610	1610
Close last trade	2/1/98	20/2/98
Closing index value	1021	1126
Net profit	1864	3645
Gross profit	3416	4303
Gross loss	-1552	-658
Number of trades	27	28
% profitable	48	64
Average profit trade	263	239
Average losing trade	-111	-66
Ratio avg. profit/avg. loss	2.4	3.6
Max. consecutive profits	2	5
Max. consecutive losses	3	3
Average weeks in profits	23	13
Average weeks in losses	10	10

Next the three different types of stops are applied as discussed in Chapter 6, and the results obtained are listed in Table 18.2 overleaf. The optimum value for the three stops is marked * in the table. It can be seen that in each case there is a broad peak of profit values, i.e. the stops are robust in that the profit is not ultra-sensitive to selecting exactly the right stop value.

The best performance is achieved with the percentage profit trailing stop with a floor set to 175 points, and a 40% retracement. A full set of values for this case is listed in column 3 of Table 18.1, where it is seen that the net profit is almost twice that achieved with no stops.

Notice that the Gold Index ends the eight-year period about 500 points lower than the start of the period, but the 28 trading legs give a net profit equivalent to 3645 points. This is what trading is all about – taking profits from the uptrends and downtrends, even though on a longer time frame the index is going nowhere.

TABLE 18.2 Results For MACD On Weekly Gold Index With Various Stops

	Net Profit	Number of Trades	Percentage Profitable
Profit Target Stop			
125 points	1848	28	71
150	2193	28	68
*175	2491	28	64
200	2351	27	59
225	2298	27	56
Dollar Trailing Stop			
100 points	2763	28	64
125	2477	27	63
*150	3016	27	67
175	2762	27	59
200	2463	27	56
Percentage Profit Trailing Stop With 175 Point Floor			
30%	3356	28	64
35	3535	28	64
*40	3645	28	64
45	3545	28	64
50	3395	28	64

*Optimum value for stop

Figure 18.1 opposite shows the weekly Gold Index with the up and down arrows marking the trades, and the arrows with the horizontal bars marking those trades which are closed on the percentage profit trailing stop (175 point floor and 40% retracement). The lower trace is the system equity which shows there was little gain during 1991/92 while the Gold Index was drifting, but from 1993 onwards the profit increased steadily as the Gold Index executed major uptrends and downtrends.

At the time of writing the only index warrant available on the Gold Index is a single call warrant which began trading on 12/1/98. From January 1998 up to the end of March 1998 there has been only one uptrend in the Gold Index as defined by the weekly MACD indicator. This trend started on 2/1/98 at 1021 points and was stopped out on 20/2/98 at 1126 points for a move of 105 points or 10%. The first day the warrant traded it closed at $1.98, and on 20/2/98 was at $2.81 for a gain of 42%. During the upward trend the warrant peaked on 29/1/98 at $3.49.

Inspection of the gold warrant chart (not shown) reveals that turnover is low and some days there are no trades. This warrant is discussed further in Chapter 22, and with the magnitude of the percentage gains available from the warrant on any upward move in the Gold Index, it is worth keeping tabs on.

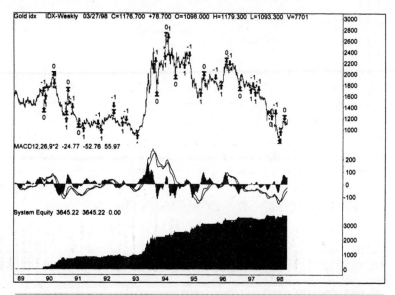

FIGURE 18.1 Weekly Gold Index With MACD And Stops

ADVANCE/DECLINE LINE

Appendix D shows the steps involved in calculating the A/D line for the AOI using Ezy Charts data and software. Similar steps are involved in calculating the A/D line for the Gold Index.

Figure 18.2(a) (overleaf) shows the daily Gold Index spanning 2.5 years, and Figure 18.2(b) (overleaf) shows the corresponding A/D line over the same time span. It is apparent from Figure 18.2(a) that the Gold Index fell steadily from March 1996 to January 1998, but is showing signs of a recovery in March 1998. The corresponding A/D line of Figure 18.2(b) shows a support line AB, and a resistance line XY. When the A/D line fell below B, further falls in the Gold Index could be anticipated. Similarly, if the A/D line moves convincingly above Y, further rises in both the A/D line and the Gold Index are likely.

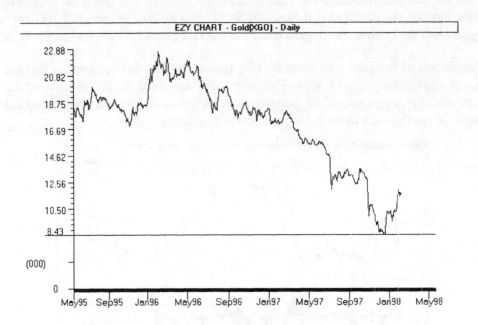

FIGURE 18.2(a)   Daily Gold Index Over 2.5 Years

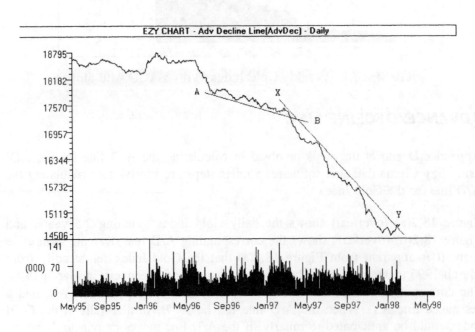

FIGURE 18.2(b)   Daily Gold Index A/D Line Over 2.5 Years

POINT & FIGURE CHARTS

Figure 18.3 shows the P&F chart for the Gold Index with a box size of 15 points and 2-box reversal. There are three congestion areas followed by breakouts on the down side, as shown at A, B and C. The chart is current to the end of April 1998, and could be making a classic head and shoulders bottom formation. If the index produces a right shoulder and then breaks above the line XY, then the P&F chart shows that the first resistance level would be around 1560 points, with the next resistance just above 1700 points.

FIGURE 18.3   Point & Figure Chart For Gold Index

111

Chapter 19

ANALYSIS OF WEEKLY ALL INDUSTRIALS INDEX

AT THE TIME OF writing there are no index warrants on the All Industrials Index trading on the ASX, though they are likely to be introduced sometime in the future.

We would expect the All Industrials Index to be more sedate in its moves and exhibit better trends than the AOI, as the AOI includes both industrial stocks and the more volatile resource stocks.

A brief analysis of the All Industrials Index is conducted using a selection of four tools, chosen to be a mix of technical indicators and charting techniques:

1. The weekly MACD indicator.

2. The Percent Model.

3. The A/D line.

4. Trend lines.

Readers with databases and software packages may like to apply some of the other technical indicators from earlier chapters to the All Industrials Index.

The weekly All Industrials Index is shown in Figure 2.5. We start by applying the weekly MACD indicator using no stops, and the results are listed in column 2 of Table 19.1 opposite, for the seven years from February 1991 to March 1998.

TABLE 19.1   Results For MACD On Weekly All Industrials Index

	MACD	325 Point Profit Target Stop	6.5 Percent Model
Open first trade	8/2/91	8/2/91	25/1/91
Opening index value	2104	2104	2008
Close last trade	9/1/98	27/3/98	27/3/98
Closing index value	4500	*4825	4741
Net profit	598	1598	2996
Gross profit	2709	3571	3460
Gross loss	-2111	-1973	-464
Number of trades	26	27	9
% profitable	42	48	67
Average profit trade	246	275	577
Average losing trade	-141	-141	-155
Ratio avg. profit/avg. loss	1.7	2.0	3.7
Max. consecutive profits	2	2	4
Max. consecutive losses	4	4	2
Average weeks in profits	21	13	57
Average weeks in losses	9	9	12

*Profit target stop triggered by intra-week high

Next the three different types of stops are applied as discussed in Chapter 6, and the results obtained are listed in Table 19.2 overleaf. The optimum value for the three stops is marked * in Table 19.2. Once again, in each case there is a broad peak of profit values, i.e. the stops are robust in that the profit is not ultra-sensitive to selecting exactly the right stop value.

The best performance is achieved with the percentage profit trailing stop with a floor set to 325 points, and a 2.5% retracement. For variety, we choose not to list the full set of values for this case, but rather select the case for a profit target stop of 325 points, and these are listed in column 3 ('325 Point Profit Target Stop') of Table 19.1. A disadvantage with the percentage profit trailing stop is that, for most stockbrokers, a new stop value needs to be given to the broker each day. In extreme cases, like the one day mini-crash of October 1997, the market needs to be monitored continuously.

TABLE 19.2 Results For MACD On Weekly All Industrials Index With Various Stops

	Net Profit	Number of Trades	Percentage Profitable
Profit Target Stop			
275 points	1207	27	48
300	1482	27	48
*325	1597	27	48
350	1377	26	46
375	1290	26	46
Dollar Trailing Stop			
125 points	1652	27	52
150	1589	27	48
175	1634	26	46
*200	1688	26	46
225	1461	26	46
Percentage Profit Trailing Stop With 325 Point Floor			
*2.5%	2047	27	48
5.0	1959	27	48
7.5	1568	26	46

*Optimum value for stop

The results for the profit target stop of 325 points show that net profit is almost three times that achieved with no stops.

Notice that the All Industrials Index ends the seven-year period about 2700 points higher than the start of the period, but the 27 trading legs give a net profit equivalent to only 1598 points. This is a disappointing result, and other indicators need be considered to improve this performance if we want to trade index-linked equities or funds (see Chapter 23) using signals from the All Industrials Index.

Figure 19.1 opposite shows the weekly All Industrials Index with the up and down arrows marking the trades, and the arrows with the horizontal bars marking those trades which are closed on the 325 point profit target stop. The lower trace is the system equity, which shows two regions marked A and B where consecutive whipsaws cut into the profits.

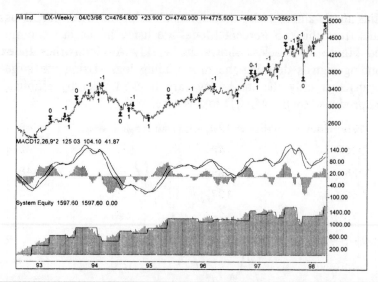

FIGURE 19.1   Weekly All Industrials Index With MACD And Stops

PERCENT MODEL

The disappointing MACD result on the weekly All Industrials Index is an incentive to try other proven trend-picking indicators. The Percent Model is a logical choice as it can be optimised to the index by changing the percentage retracement value. Table 19.3 lists the profit results for a range of percentage retracements, over the same time span as used in Table 19.1.

TABLE 19.3   Results For Percent Model On Weekly All Industrials Index

Percentage Retracement	Net Profit	Number of Trades	Percentage Profitable
4.0%	1733	23	43
4.5	2016	19	47
5.0	2438	15	53
5.5	2682	13	62
6.0	2819	11	64
*6.5	2996	9	67
7.0	2714	9	67

*Optimum percentage retracement

These results show that as the percentage retracement is increased the number of trades falls while the net profit increases. With 6.5% retracement the net profit is

115

2996 points and is almost twice the best result achieved with MACD using stops. The results from this 6.5 Percent Model are listed in the last column of Table 19.1, and Figure 19.2 below shows the weekly All Industrials Index and the corresponding signals defining the nine trading legs. Using the large value of 6.5% means that only the major legs are tracked, thereby eliminating many whipsaws produced by the MACD in this case.

FIGURE 19.2   Weekly All Industrials Index With 6.5 Percent Model Signals

If index warrants become available on the All Industrials Index, their gearing and profitability need to be investigated in order to determine profitable trading strategies capitalising on the long trends available.

ADVANCE/DECLINE LINE

Figure 19.3(a) (opposite) shows the daily All Industrials Index spanning 2.5 years, and Figure 19.3(b) (opposite) shows the corresponding daily A/D line. For some 20 months to July 1997, the index and the A/D line demonstrate togetherness, by tracking up and down in unison. However, from July to October 1997, the index higher highs A,B,C are accompanied by divergence X,Y,Z in the A/D line, thereby warning of a fall in the index. In March 1998 the new higher high marked D in the index is accompanied by another lower A/D line value (see L), which further warns that sometime in the future the index will fall.

It is stressed that divergence between the index and the A/D line is not a timing signal, but rather is a warning sign of a change in direction of the index trend.

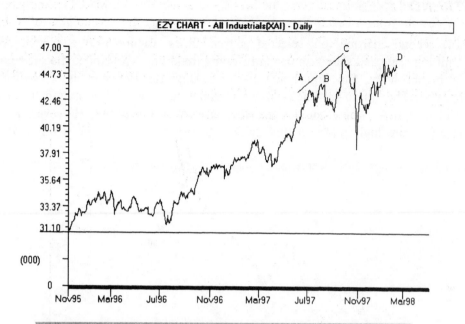

FIGURE 19.3(a)   Daily All Industrials Index Over 2.5 Years

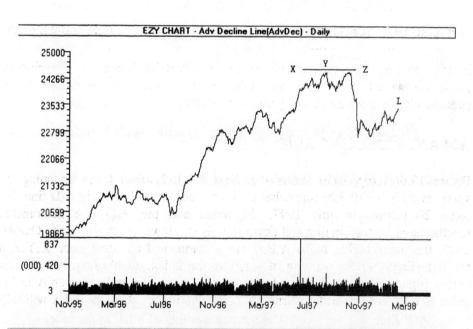

FIGURE 19.3(b)   Daily All Industrials Index A/D Line Over 2.5 Years

TREND LINES

The second charting tool selected is trend lines. Figure 19.4 is plotted on a semi-log scale and shows an upward sloping trend line XX. Notice the succession of higher highs and higher lows, which Dow theory states is a confirmed uptrend. The horizontal line is drawn to show that trough B is marginally lower than trough A, which could signal the onset of a downtrend. However, prices rose to a new high in March 1998 so Dow theory says the uptrend is still intact.

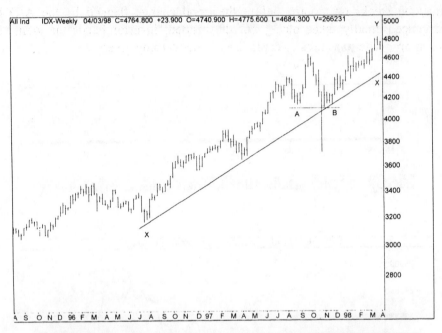

FIGURE 19.4   Weekly All Industrials Index With Trend Lines

FOUR TOOLS – BUT WHAT RESULT?

At the end of March 1998 the four different analysis methods give the following results on the weekly All Industrials Index:

MACD	Uptrend stopped out at profit target
Percent Model	Uptrend still in force
A/D Line	Divergence warning of a fall in the index
Trend Line	Uptrend still in force

The 6.5 Percent Model and the trend line analysis are both telling us the uptrend is still in force. However, the MACD is saying "careful", as its uptrend has been stopped out at the 325 point profit target. The A/D line is more insistent, as the divergence with the index is positively shouting "CAREFUL!"

So we have the conundrum faced by technical analysts. Two indicators are saying up, but two others are warning to be careful. What the future holds, only time will tell.

It may be weeks or months before the trend change flagged by the A/D line divergence actually takes place, but the prudent investor heeds the signs, and takes appropriate measures to capitalise on the warning given.

Chapter 20

ANALYSIS OF WEEKLY
ALL RESOURCES INDEX

AT THE TIME of writing there are no index warrants on the All Resources Index trading on the ASX, though they are likely to be introduced sometime in the future.

We would expect the All Resources Index to be volatile, as the heavyweight resource stocks are more volatile than the heavyweight industrial stocks.

A brief analysis of the All Resources Index is conducted using the three tools:

1. The weekly MACD indicator.

2. The A/D line.

3. Trend lines.

The weekly All Resources Index is shown in Figure 2.6. Once again, we start by applying the weekly MACD indicator using no stops, and the results are listed in column 2 of Table 20.1 opposite, for the 7.5 years from September 1990 to February 1998.

TABLE 20.1 Results For MACD On Weekly All Resources Index

	MACD	Floor 200 Point Percent 12.5
Open first trade	21/9/90	21/9/90
Opening index value	895	895
Close last trade	23/1/98	31/10/97
Closing index value	1122	1062
Net profit	467	777
Gross profit	1289	1599
Gross loss	-822	-822
Number of trades	31	31
% profitable	42	42
Average profit trade	99	123
Average losing trade	-46	-46
Ratio avg. profit/avg. loss	2.2	2.7
Max. consecutive profits	2	2
Max. consecutive losses	6	6
Average weeks in profits	21	18
Average weeks in losses	6	6

Next the three different types of stops are applied as discussed in Chapter 6, and the results obtained are listed in Table 20.2 overleaf.

It is interesting to note that dollar trailing stops do not improve the basic MACD results. (This conclusion was reached with the weekly AOI also.)

The optimum value for the other two stops is marked * in Table 20.2, and in each case there is a broad peak of profit values, i.e. the stops are robust in that the profit is not ultra-sensitive to selecting exactly the right stop value.

The best performance is achieved with the percentage profit trailing stop with a floor set to 200 points, and a 12.5% retracement. The full set of profit results for this case is listed in the last column of Table 20.1, and show that net profit is about 67% higher than that achieved with no stops.

TABLE 20.2 Results For MACD On Weekly All Resources Index With Various Stops

	Net Profit	Number of Trades	Percentage Profitable
Profit Target Stop			
150 points	597	31	42
175	533	31	42
*200	658	31	42
225	477	31	42
250	552	31	42
Dollar Trailing Stop			
50 points	No improvement on basic MACD results		
...			
...			
200			
Percentage Profit Trailing Stop With 200 Point Floor			
7.5%	659	31	42
10.0	636	31	42
*12.5	777	31	42
15.0	750	31	42
17.5	722	31	42

*Optimum value for stop

Notice that the All Resources Index ends the 7.5 year period only about 230 points higher than the start of the period, but the 31 trading legs give a net profit equivalent to 777 points.

A second point to note is that the MACD indicator applied to the weekly AOI over the same 7.5 years gives 23 trades of which 52% are correct (see Table 6.1). Thus, by comparison, the All Resources Index is not particularly amenable to analysis by the trend-following weekly MACD. Other indicators like Stochastic and Relative Strength which are more suited to oscillating behaviour could be considered.

Figure 20.1 opposite shows the weekly All Resources Index with the up and down arrows marking the trades, and the arrows with the horizontal bars marking those trades which are closed on the percentage profit target stop with floor of 200 points and 12.5% retracement. The lower trace is the system equity which shows the majority of the profit came from the single downtrend trade culminating in the October 1997 mini-crash.

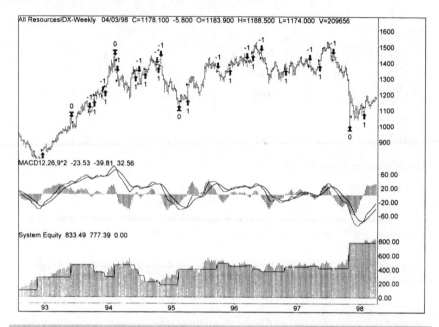

FIGURE 20.1   Weekly All Resources Index With MACD And Stops

Inspection of Figure 2.4 for the Gold Index, and Figure 2.6 for the All Resources Index, reveals that they are both obviously volatile. Thus we would expect them both to produce trading profits. Yet the analysis with weekly MACD shows the Gold Index gives excellent results, whereas the All Resources Index does not. This demonstrates the need to do our own analysis to confirm ideas and hunches, and once again shows the usefulness of back-testing.

ADVANCE/DECLINE LINE

Figure 20.2(a) (overleaf) shows the daily All Resources Index spanning 2.5 years, and Figure 20.2(b) (overleaf) shows the corresponding daily A/D line. Regions A and C on the index are two equal peaks, while region B is a valley separating them. On the A/D line chart, the corresponding regions are X, P and Y. We see that line YP is at a marked divergence to line BC, and P is well below X. This divergence signals a continuing fall in the index as it turns down from the peak C.

123

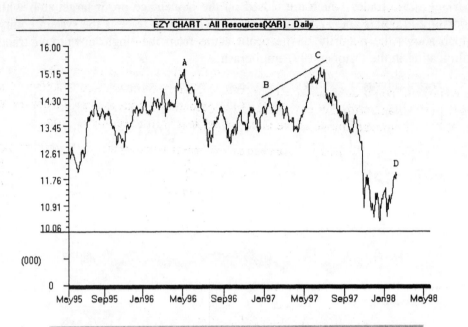

FIGURE 20.2(a)   Daily All Resources Index Over 2.5 Years

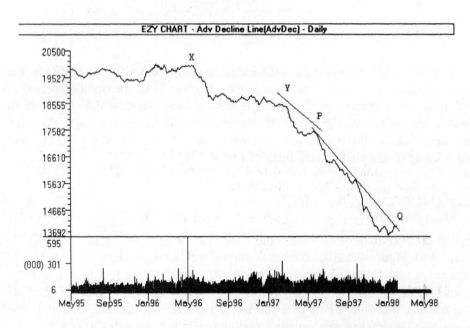

FIGURE 20.2(b)   Daily All Resources Index A/D Line Over 2.5 Years

Another use of the A/D line is the application of trend lines. The trend line PQ in Figure 20.2(b) is penetrated in February 1998, and suggests an upward move in the index, which is confirmed at D in Figure 20.2(a).

TREND LINES

Figure 20.3 is plotted on a semi-log scale and shows two upward-sloping trend lines which start at point A. The index penetrates line AB at C, and then continues to fall.

Similarly, line AX is penetrated at Y, but the index reverses and retests the trend line before continuing the downtrend. This is a classic signal, and when the index starts to fall after retesting the trend line, the downtrend is confirmed.

FIGURE 20.3   Weekly All Resources Index With Trend Lines

Part III

FINANCIAL PRODUCTS

Chapter 21

INDEX WARRANTS - DEFINITIONS AND OFFERINGS

INDEX WARRANTS BEGAN trading on the ASX on Monday 12 January 1998. Three companies offered a variety of call and put warrants on the AOI, plus a single call warrant on the Gold Index. At that time the AOI was around 2550 points and the Gold Index was around 950 points.

Before looking into the details of these warrants, some warrant terminology needs to be presented. Index warrants are similar in concept to warrants and exchange traded options on shares. However, for index warrants the underlying security is a basket of shares in companies that comprise the index, with the number of shares in each company in the basket being weighted in the same proportion as the weighting used in the index.

At February 1998 there were some 299 companies included in the AOI, and 27 companies in the Gold Index.

Index Call Warrants

A purchase of index call warrants will increase in value if the index goes up. At expiry time, if the index is above the exercise level, then settlement is in cash. Alternatively, if a large number of warrants are held, settlement can be in the basket of shares comprising the index at that time.

Each of the companies offering index warrants have differing cash settlement conditions which are discussed below.

If the index is below the exercise level at expiry, then the call index warrants expire worthless.

Index Put Warrants

A purchase of index put warrants will increase in value if the index goes down. At expiry time, if the index is below the exercise level, then settlement is in cash. Alternatively, if a large number of warrants are held, settlement can be in the basket of shares comprising the index at that time.

If the index is above the exercise level at expiry, then the put index warrants expire worthless.

Expiry Date

The expiry date is the last day on which an index warrant can be exercised. When the warrants are first issued, the expiry dates range from typically 9 months to 20 months.

American-Style

American-style index warrants can be exercised at any time up to the expiry date.

European-Style

European-style index warrants can only be exercised on the expiry date.

Exercise Level

The AOI call warrants have exercise levels in the range 2400 to 3200, while the AOI put warrants have exercise levels in the range 2000 to 2600.

The Gold Index call warrant has an exercise level of 1000.

(The term "exercise level" as used with index warrants has the same meaning as "strike price" or "exercise price" used with options.)

At-the-money, In-the-money, Out-of-the-money

The left-hand side of Table 21.1 below shows a series of index call warrants with the index at 2500. The warrant with an exercise level of 2500 is called "at-the-money", the warrant with an exercise level of 2600 or above is called "out-of-the-money", while the warrant with an exercise level of 2400 or below is called "in-the-money".

The right-hand side of Table 21.1 shows a series of index put warrants with the index also at 2500. The warrant with an exercise level of 2500 is called "at-the-money", the warrant with an exercise level of 2400 or below is called "out-of-the-money", while the warrant with an exercise level of 2600 or above is called "in-the-money".

TABLE 21.1 Call And Put Index Warrants With Index Exercise Level of 2500

CALL WARRANTS	Index Exercise Level	PUT WARRANTS
Out-of-the-money	– – – – 2800 – – – – – – – – 2600 – – – –	In-the-money
At-the-money	– – – – 2500 – – – –	At-the-money
In-the-money	– – – – 2400 – – – – – – – – 2300 – – – –	Out-of-the-money

Contract Size

The ASX trading rules allows just one warrant to be traded. However, index warrant trades are usually in multiples of 500 or 1,000.

Conversion Ratio, Multiplying Factor, Index Exposure

The conversion ratio is the number of index warrants needed to make up one unit of the index. The multiplying factor is the number used to convert the warrants to a dollar value on the index. The index exposure is the nominal dollar value of the index controlled by one warrant.

131

Comparing warrant prices and gearing is made difficult because each of the three offering companies has different conversion ratios, multiplying factors and index exposures, and in some cases call them by different names. In the discussions below, we try to compare apples with apples, and try to standardise the various warrant parameters.

Index Warrant Quotations

Index warrants are quoted daily in *The Australian* and *The Australian Financial Review*, but not generally in the local newspapers.

The segment shown in Figure 21.1 is from *The Australian* and the column headings are local code, ASX index warrant code, exercise level, expiry date, conversion ratio, buyer quote, seller quote, last sale price, number of warrants traded that day in 100s.

AOI   2799 pts   GOLD INDEX   1096 pts

All Ordinaries Index - Call Warrants
All Ords

9087	XAOWMA	2400	30/09/98	1:1	5.08	5.15	5.10	210
9088	XAOWMB	2800	31/12/98	1:1	3.17	3.21	2.69	
9079	XAOWDA	2800	31/03/99	500:1	.76	.78	.71	
9080	XAOWDB	3000	30/06/99	500:1	.65	.67	.65	30
9081	XAOWDC	3200	30/06/99	500:1	.51	.54		
9084	XAOWSA	2500	30/09/99	1:1	2.37	2.43	2.05	
9085	XAOWSB	2600	30/09/99	1:1	2.17	2.23	2.21	14
9086	XAOWSC	2700	30/09/99	1:1	1.98	2.04	1.78	

Gold Index - Call Warrants
Gold Index

9091	XGOWMA	1000	31/12/98	1:1	2.45	2.65	2.70	

All Ordinaries Index - Put Warrants
All Ords

9090	XAOWMQ	2600	30/09/98	1:1	1.68	1.71	1.70	3084
9089	XAOWMP	2200	31/12/98	1:1	1.12	1.16	1.17	
9082	XAOWDP	2250	31/03/99	500:1	.30½	.32	.31	100
9083	XAOWDQ	2000	30/06/99	500:1	.21½	.24½	.26	

FIGURE 21.1   INDEX WARRANT QUOTES ON 23/3/98

Trading Index Warrants

Index warrants are traded on the ASX through the Stock Exchange Automated Trading System (SEATS) screen trading system, and are cleared via the Clearing House Electronic Sub-register System (CHESS), in exactly the same way as for shares.

Making a Market

Each of the three offering companies make a market on their own index warrants. This means there is always a buyer and a seller for each warrant, though the buyer/seller quotes may sometimes be wide, depending on the activity in that warrant.

Only the offering companies are allowed to issue index warrants, i.e. sell them to the public, but once issued the index warrants can be bought and sold just like shares up to their expiry time. (The exception to this trading is that the public cannot short sell warrants – see Chapter 25.)

Brokerage on Index Warrants

Index warrants are treated by stockbrokers like any other security, with some charging on a percentage basis while others charge a fixed fee. The cut-price broker Green Line Investor Services (previously Pont Securities), phone 1300 653 133, have a fixed scale of fees. The costs to open or close an index warrant trade are:

Trade Value ($)	0-14,999	15,000-49,999	50,000-79,999	>80,000
Brokerage ($)	60	70	80	0.1%

A "full service" broker charges typically 1.5% to 2.5% commission on the parcel value to open or close an index warrant trade, with a minimum of typically $35. Many brokers are now offering reduced commissions for orders placed via email or the Internet, with minimum brokerage typically $30. The monthly magazines *Shares* and *Personal Investment* carry many advertisements from discount brokers.

There is one difference between trades in shares and index warrants, in that there is no stamp duty to pay in the case of index warrants.

Deposits and Margin Calls

Prior to purchasing index warrants, the necessary cash must be lodged with the broker. After the purchase is made there are no margin calls. If the value of the index moves against the holder, then their investment falls in value and could even fall to zero, but there would be no margin calls nor further deposits required.

PRICING THE WARRANT

The price of an index warrant comprises the intrinsic value plus the time premium as:

Warrant price = intrinsic value + time premium

Intrinsic Value

The intrinsic value is the amount the warrant is worth if it were to expire today (talking into account the conversion ratio, exercise level and multiplying factors).

Time Premium

The time premium on an index warrant is the additional value of the warrant above the intrinsic value, and takes into account the time to expiry and some other market variables which are discussed in Chapter 22.

At-the-money and out-of-the-money put and call warrants have a time premium but no intrinsic value.

The time premium is a wasting asset. For both put and call warrants, as the time to expiry shortens, the time premium falls linearly until about the last four weeks when it begins to fall more steeply (see Chapter 22).

MACQUARIE BANK INDEX WARRANTS

The Macquarie Bank (Macquarie for short) index warrants are listed below.

ASX CODE	Style	Call or Put	Exercise Level	Expiry Date
All Ordinaries Index				
XAOWMA	Euro	Call	2400	30.9.98
XAOWMB	Euro	Call	2800	31.12.98
XAOWMQ	Euro	Put	2600	30.9.98
XAOWMP	Euro	Put	2200	31.12.98
Gold Index				
XGOWMA	Am	Call	1000	31.12.98

Notice that the call and put index warrants on the AOI are all European-style, while the call index warrant on the Gold Index is American-style.

Intrinsic Value

The Macquarie index warrants have a conversion ratio of 1:1 and a multiplying factor of 1¢ or $0.01. Thus the intrinsic value of one call warrant is:

Intrinsic value = (index value – exercise level) × 0.01 dollars

Thus if the AOI is trading at 2650 points, the intrinsic value of the call warrant with an exercise level of 2400 is:

Intrinsic value = (2650 – 2400) × 0.01 = $2.50

Index Exposure

Each warrant is linked to the underlying index with a multiplier of $0.01. Thus for a warrant with an exercise level of 2400 the index exposure of the warrant is:

Index exposure = 2400 × 0.01 = $24.00

The nexus between the warrant and the index is that one warrant gives exposure to 24 points of index.

The index exposure value is used in Chapter 22 to calculate the theoretical price of the warrant.

Cash Settlement Amount

At expiry, warrants which are in-the-money will have a cash settlement. Suppose at expiry the AOI is 2700. For a call warrant with an exercise level of 2400 the cash value of the warrant is:

Cash value = (2700 – 2400) × 0.01 = $3.00

If we hold 1,000 AOI warrants with an exercise level of 2400, and at expiry the index is 2700 points, then the value of the parcel of warrants is:

Parcel value = 1000 × (2700 – 2400) × 0.01 = $3,000

A profit accrues if this cash settlement value is greater than the initial purchase price of the warrants.

It is not necessary to wait to expiry to quit the warrants, as they can be sold on the ASX at the market price, any time up to the expiry date.

Alternatively, if we have 2,000 Gold Index warrants with an exercise level of 1000, and at expiry the index is 1200 points, then the value of the parcel of warrants is:

$$\text{Parcel value} = 2000 \times (1200 - 1000) \times 0.01 = \$4{,}000$$

Once again, the resulting profit is the difference between $4,000 and the purchase cost of the 2,000 index warrants.

DEUTSCHE BANK AG INDEX WARRANTS

The Deutsche Bank AG (DB for short) index warrants are listed below.

ASX CODE	Style	Call or Put	Exercise Level	Expiry Date
All Ordinaries Index				
XAOWDA	Euro	Call	2800	31.3.99
XAOWDB	Euro	Call	3000	30.6.99
XAOWDC	Euro	Call	3200	30.6.99
XAOWDP	Euro	Put	2250	31.3.99
XAOWDQ	Euro	Put	2000	30.6.99

The call and put index warrants on the AOI are all European-style, and have longer expiry times than the Macquarie index warrants.

Intrinsic Value

The DB index warrants have a conversion ratio of 500:1. A move of one point in the index translates to a move of $1 per 500 warrants. Thus the intrinsic value of one call warrant is:

$$\text{Intrinsic value} = (\text{index value} - \text{exercise level}) \times \frac{1}{500} \text{ dollars}$$

Thus if the AOI is trading at 3050 points, the intrinsic value of the call warrant with exercise level 2800 is:

$$\text{Intrinsic value} = (3050 - 2800) \times \frac{1}{500} = \$0.50$$

Index Exposure

Each warrant is linked to the underlying index with a multiplier of $\frac{1}{500} = \$0.002$. Thus, for a warrant with an exercise level of 2800 the index exposure of the warrant is:

$$\text{Index exposure} = 2800 \times 0.002 = \$5.60$$

The nexus between the warrant and the index is that one warrant gives exposure to 5.6 points of index.

Cash Settlement Amount

At expiry, warrants which are in-the-money will have a cash settlement. Suppose at expiry the AOI is 3100. For a call warrant with an exercise level of 2800 the cash value of the warrant is:

$$\text{Cash value} = \frac{(3100 - 2800)}{500} = \$0.60$$

If we hold 1,000 AOI warrants with an exercise level of 2800, and at expiry the index is 3100 points, then the value of the parcel of warrants is:

$$\text{Parcel value} = 1000 \times (3100 - 2800) \times \frac{1}{500} = \$600$$

A profit accrues if this cash settlement value is greater than the initial purchase price of the warrant.

Once again, the warrants can be sold on the ASX at the market price, any time up to the expiry date.

SBG WARBURG DILLON READ INDEX WARRANTS

The SBG Warburg Dillon Read (SBG for short) index warrants are listed below.

ASX CODE	Style	Call or Put	Exercise Level	Expiry Date
All Ordinaries Index				
XAOWSA	Am	Call	2500	30.9.99
XAOWSB	Am	Call	2600	30.9.99
XAOWSC	Am	Call	2700	30.9.99

Only call warrants on the AOI are available, and they are American-style, having all expiry dates on the same day, which is later than either the Macquarie or DB index warrants.

Intrinsic Value

The SBG index warrants have a conversion ratio of 1:1 and a multiplying factor of $0.004. A move of one point in the index translates to a move of $0.004 per warrant. Thus the intrinsic value of one call warrant is:

Intrinsic value = (index value – exercise level) $\times$ 0.004 dollars

Thus if the AOI is trading at 2850 points, the intrinsic value of the call warrant with exercise level 2600 is:

Intrinsic value = (2850 – 2600) $\times$ 0.004 = $1.00

Index Exposure

Each warrant is linked to the underlying index with a multiplier of $0.004. Thus for a warrant with an exercise level of 2600 the index exposure of the warrant is:

Index exposure = 2600 $\times$ 0.004 = $10.40

The nexus between the warrant and the index is that one warrant gives exposure to 10.4 points of index.

Cash Settlement Amount

At expiry, warrants which are in-the-money will have a cash settlement. Suppose at expiry the All Ordinaries Index is 3100. For a call warrant with an exercise level of 2800 the cash value of the warrant is:

$$\text{Cash value} = (3100 - 2800) \times 0.004 = \$1.20$$

If we hold 1,000 AOI warrants with an exercise level of 2800, and at expiry the index is 3100 points, then the value of the parcel of warrants is:

$$\text{Parcel value} = 1000 \times (3100 - 2800) \times 0.004 = \$1,200$$

A profit accrues if this cash settlement value is greater than the initial purchase price of the warrants.

As before, the warrants can be sold on the ASX at the market price, any time up to the expiry date.

WARRANT OFFERING CIRCULAR

Given the lack of standardisation between the index warrants from the three offering companies, investors are advised to obtain a copy of the relevant Offering Circular before making a purchase. The various warrant definitions must be properly understood, along with the relevant conversion ratios, multiplying factors and index exposures, so investors know exactly what is being purchased. If in doubt, discuss the warrant details with a stockbroker, or the issuer of the warrant.

If we buy call index warrants and the market moves down we could lose our investment. Similarly, if we buy put index warrants and the market moves up we could lose our investment. Thus, prior to the first purchase of warrants it is necessary to sign a form with our broker to the effect that the risks associated with warrant transactions are understood.

The next chapter discusses how to calculate the theoretical price of index warrants, the factors which influence their price, and how to select the appropriate warrant for a trade.

Chapter 22

PRICING INDEX WARRANTS

TO TRADE WARRANTS confidently it is necessary to understand the mechanics of warrant pricing, and how warrants respond to market forces.

The factors that influence the price of an index warrant are:

1. Index level.

2. Warrant exercise level.

3. Time to expiry.

4. Risk-free interest rate for the same length of time as the warrant expiry.

5. Volatility of the index.

6. Underlying mood of the market.

Some of these factors are listed in Table 22.1, along with their effect upon the warrant price.

TABLE 22.1   Index Warrant Response To Market Factors

Market Variable	Change in Variable	Warrant Price Change	
		Call	Put
Index level	Up	Up	Down
Time to expiry	Shorter	Down	Down
Volatility	Up	Up	Up
Interest rates	Up	Up	Down
Dividend expectations	Up	Down	Up

Trading Stock Options and Warrants investigates the relative option and warrant price changes for changes in the market variables, and shows that volatility is the dominant variable. This topic is discussed later in this chapter.

THE BLACK-SCHOLES OPTION PRICING MODEL

There are a number of mathematical formulae used to calculate the fair price of an option or warrant. One popular formulation is that developed by Black and Scholes, and we confine our discussion to this Black-Scholes Option Pricing Model (BSOPM) for calculating the price of index warrants.

The model is defined, and then used to calculate the price of an AOI call warrant. For index warrants Lee, Finnerty and Worth show the warrant price is a function of the parameters:

S = current index level equated to dollars

X = warrant exercise level equated to dollars

T = time to expiry in years

r = risk-less interest rate for the same time duration as the warrant expiry

v = volatility of the index

The BSOPM assumes the warrant is held to expiry, and dividends do not effect the level of the index.

For call warrants the BSOPM value C is:

$$C = S\,N(d_1) - Xe^{-rT}\,N(d_2)$$

For put warrants the BSOPM value P is:

$$P = -S\,N(-d_1) + Xe^{-rT}\,N(-d_2)$$

where:

$$d_1 = \frac{ln\left(\frac{S}{X}\right) + \left(r + \frac{v^2}{2}\right)T}{v\sqrt{T}}$$

$$d_2 = d_1 - v\sqrt{T}$$

Further:

$N()$ = the cumulative normal distribution

e = the exponential = 2.718

ln = the natural logarithm

The volatility v is defined as the square root of the annualised variance v^2.

To calculate the annualised variance, firstly the arithmetic mean, m, of the daily compounded return is determined over, say, 30 days as:

$$m = \frac{1}{30} \sum_{t=1}^{30} ln\left(\frac{P_t}{P_{t-1}}\right) = \frac{1}{30} ln\left(\frac{P_{30}}{P_0}\right)$$

and:

P_t and P_{t-1} are index levels on day t and t-1 respectively

$\left(\frac{P_t}{P_{t-1}}\right) = R_t$ the daily holding period return on the index

The annualised variance v^2 is:

$$v^2 = 365 \times \frac{1}{30-1} \sum_{t=1}^{30} (ln\, R_t - m)^2$$

Whence:

$$volatility = \sqrt{v^2} = v$$

By convention, volatility is expressed as a percentage. Thus if the annualised variance = 0.09, then the volatility = 0.30 which equates to 30%.

HISTORIC, FUTURE AND IMPLIED VOLATILITY

The BSOPM uses five parameters to calculate the warrant price. The index level, exercise level, time to expiry and risk-free interest rate are readily known, but finding the correct value for volatility is less certain.

The volatility formula above uses past data for its calculation, so this is referred to as "historic volatility". A problem arises in that different data sample lengths result in different values for the historic volatility. A second problem is that a better estimate of the warrant price would come from using the "future volatility", i.e. the index volatility from now to the warrant expiry. Of course, we do not know if the volatility in the future will be the same as the volatility in the past.

To overcome this problem it is customary to use "implied volatility", which is the market's estimate of the future volatility, to calculate the warrant price. Thus we select a particular index and a number of warrant series with different exercise levels and expiry times. We then equate the BSOPM prices to the various market warrant prices, and solve iteratively to obtain the volatility values. These volatility values should be close to one another, and the average becomes the implied volatility being used by the market. This implied volatility can then be used to calculate other warrant series prices, which will be close to the market value.

Example of Calculating All Ordinaries Index Warrant Price

The BSOPM formula is used to calculate the value of a Macquarie AOI call warrant. Input data is AOI 2656 points, warrant index level 2400, time to expiry 237 days, risk-less rate 5.0%, and the implied volatility estimated as 31%.

Chapter 21 shows the index exposure for this Macquarie warrant (XAOWMA) is 24 points, or a dollar value of $24.00. Similarly, the dollar value of the AOI is $26.56.

The BSOPM call option value C is calculated using:

S = $26.56

X = $24.00

T = time to maturity = 237 days = 0.6493 years

r = 0.05, i.e. 5.0%

v = 31% = 0.31 and v^2 = 0.0961

Then:

$$d_1 = \frac{ln\left(\frac{26.56}{24.00}\right) + \left(0.05 + \frac{0.0961}{2}\right) \times 0.6493}{0.31\sqrt{0.6493}}$$

$$= \frac{0.10135 + 0.06366}{0.2498}$$

$$= 0.6606$$

and:

$$d_2 = 0.6606 - 0.2498$$

$$= 0.4108$$

Whence:

$$N(d_1) = 0.746$$

$$N(d_2) = 0.659$$

$$e^{-rT} = e^{-0.05 \times 0.6493} = 0.968$$

The BSOPM call warrant price C is:

$$C = 26.56 \times 0.746 - 24.00 \times 0.968 \times 0.659$$

$$= \$4.50$$

IMPLIED VOLATILITY OF INDICES

Table 22.2 opposite gives a snapshot of index warrant prices on 23/3/98. The AOI closed at 2779 points and was up four points on the day, so it was a steady day. About half the index warrants were traded (see Figure 21.1), but the buyer/seller quotes of the untraded warrants were within a few cents of each other, so a mid-point value can be taken as pseudo trades. The warrant prices are listed in column 5 of Table 22.2. Using these prices in the BSOPM of SuperCharts 4, it is possible to calculate the AOI volatility being used in the BSOPM for each warrant – the volatilities are listed in column 6. The risk-free interest rate is set at 5%.

Column 4 of Table 22.2 is the index exposure for each warrant expressed in dollars, and is the parameter X in the BSOPM. The dollar value of the AOI for Macquarie, DB and SBG is $27.79, $5.56 and $11.12 respectively, and is the parameter S in the BSOPM.

On 23/3/98 the Gold Index closed at 1096 points, giving a dollar value of 10.96 for calculating the Gold Index volatility, while the single gold warrant has an index level of 1000, giving a dollar index exposure of $10.00.

TABLE 22.2   Index Warrant Prices, Volatility And Delta

ASX Code	Exercise Level	Expiry Date	Index Exposure ($)	Warrant Price (¢) 23/3/98	Volume (%)	Warrant Price (¢) 5/2/98	Delta (¢)
All Ordinaries Index Calls							123 Pt Delta
XAOWMA	2400	30.9.98	24.00	510	30	447	63
XAOWMB	2800	31.12.98	28.00	319	29	275	44
XAOWDA	2800	31.3.99	5.60	77	29	61	16
XAOWDB	3000	30.6.99	6.00	66	27	55	11
XAOWDC	3200	30.6.99	6.40	52	28	45	7
XAOWSA	2500	30.9.99	10.00	240	25	214	26
XAOWSB	2600	30.9.99	10.40	220	26	196	24
XAOWSC	2700	30.9.99	10.80	201	27	178	23
All Ordinaries Index Puts							
XAOWMQ	2600	30.9.98	26.00	170	36	247	-77
XAOWMP	2200	31.12.98	22.00	114	41	165	-51
XAOWDP	2250	31.3.99	4.50	31	40	39	-8
XAOWDQ	2000	30.6.99	4.00	23	41	30	-7
Gold Index Call							-70 Pt Delta
XGOWMA	1000	31.12.98	10.00	255	50	315	-60

Table 22.2 shows that for the AOI call warrants, the volatility values across the various classes of warrants range from 25% to 30%, with a mean value of around 28%.

The AOI put warrants are seen to have higher volatility values of 36% to 41%. This is possibly due to an expectation that the market is likely to fall, because of the uncertainty associated with the then-current Asian crisis.

The single Gold Index warrant has a very high volatility of 50%.

By way of comparison, the volatility values on exchange traded options (on BHP, NAB, etc.) and equity warrants is typically 15% to 30%, with industrial stocks having lower volatilities and resource stocks having higher volatilities.

INDEX WARRANT DELTA

For equity warrants and options on stocks, delta is defined as:

Delta = change in warrant or option price for a +1 point change in stock price

In the case of index warrants, the conversion factors and multiplying factors (*MF*) need be taken into account in determining delta.

$$\text{Index warrant delta} = \frac{1}{MF} \times \frac{\text{change in warrant price in dollars}}{\text{change in index value in points}}$$

Thus Macquarie warrants with a multiplying factor of 0.01 have a delta of 1, if a 1 point move in the index changes the warrant price by 1¢. Similarly, DB warrants with a multiplying factor of 0.002 have a delta of 1, if a 1 point move in the index changes the warrant price by 0.2¢. For SBG warrants the corresponding warrant move is 0.4¢.

Using these multipliers, theoretical values of delta for the various index warrants can be calculated from the BSOPM.

However, rather than use theoretical delta values, it is more useful to measure the actual change in warrant price for, say, a given point move of the index, as this is what is happening on the market. On 5/2/98 the AOI closed at 2656 points and the Gold Index closed at 1166 points. The corresponding actual index warrant prices were as listed in column 7 in Table 22.2. From 5/2/98 to 23/3/98 the AOI rose 123 points, and the Gold Index fell 70 points. The last column of Table 22.2 is the difference between column 5 and column 7, and is the actual warrant move for the 123-point rise in the AOI, or the 70-point fall in the Gold Index.

We define the term "practical delta" as:

$$\text{Practical delta} = \frac{\text{change in warrant price in cents}}{\text{index move in points}}$$

For the first Macquarie call index warrant in Table 22.2 the practical delta is $\frac{63}{123} = 0.51$, which means that for a 1 point rise in the AOI the warrant moves 0.51¢. Similarly, the first DB call warrant practical delta is $\frac{16}{123} = 0.13$, and the first SBG call warrant practical delta is $\frac{26}{123} = 0.21$.

GEARING

For warrants on stocks, gearing is a term used to describe the ratio of profit to be made through buying a parcel of warrants compared with a similar value parcel of shares.

In the case of index warrants, a question arises as to what is the price of the index, and can we buy the index? Chapter 23 discusses the Benchmark Australian All Ordinaries Index Trust (BAT), a share investment fund which invests in a portfolio replicating the companies in the AOI. The BAT trades on the ASX and tracks the value of the AOI very closely using a multiplier of 0.01. Thus when the AOI is, say, 2656 points, the BAT price is about $26.56.

We define gearing for the index call warrants as:

$$\text{Gearing} = \frac{\text{profit on parcel of index warrants}}{\text{profit on parcel of BAT shares}}$$

where both parcels have the same initial dollar value.

As an example, consider the first Macquarie call warrant listed in Table 22.2 priced at $4.47 on 5/2/98 when the AOI was 2656 points. Assuming the BAT was priced at $26.56 then for an outlay of $2,656 we could buy 100 BAT shares or 594 warrants. On 23/3/98 the AOI had risen 123 points to 2779 points, while the warrant had risen to 63¢ to $5.10. Thus the profit on the BAT is $123 while the profit on the warrants is $594 \times 0.63 = \$374$, giving a gearing of $\frac{374}{123} = 3.0$.

The gearing for each of the index call warrants is given in the last column of Table 22.3 overleaf, and are seen to vary from 2.6 to 5.7.

WHICH INDEX WARRANT GIVES THE BEST RETURN?

Table 22.3 lists the index call warrants with their prices on 5/2/98 and 23/3/98, which allows the returns from each warrant to be calculated.

Suppose we spent $5,000 on each of the index call warrants on 5/2/98 with prices as listed in column 3 of Table 22.3. Column 4 of Table 22.3 gives the number of each warrant that can be bought for $5,000 (ignoring brokerage), while column 6 gives the profit on each parcel of warrants if they are sold on 23/3/98 after the AOI rises 123 points.

The corresponding profit on a $5,000 parcel of BAT shares is:

$$\text{Profit} = \frac{5000}{26.56} \times 1.23 = \$231$$

TABLE 22.3 Profit On A $5,000 Parcel Of Call Warrants

ASX Code	Exercise Level	Warrant Price (¢) 5/2/98	No. of Warrants 23/3/98	Warrant Price (¢) 23/3/98	Profit	Gearing
All Ordinaries Index Calls						
XAOWMA	2400	447	1,118	510	704	3.0
XAOWMB	2800	275	1,818	319	800	3.5
*XAOWDA	2800	61	8,196	77	1,311	5.7
XAOWDB	3000	55	9,090	66	1,000	4.3
XAOWDC	3200	45	11,111	52	778	3.4
XAOWSA	2500	214	2,336	240	607	2.6
XAOWSB	2600	196	2,551	220	612	2.6
XAOWSC	2700	178	2,808	201	646	2.8

*Largest profit and gearing obtained

Table 22.3 shows that there is considerable variation in the actual profit from the various warrants. The first DB warrant (marked *) gives the largest profit and gearing.

The variation in profit is caused by the fundamental properties of warrant risk/reward behaviour, i.e.:

• Warrants with the same time to expiry always have their highest time premium when they are at-the-money.

• Warrants with longer time to expiry give lower profits than those with short time to expiry, all other factors being equal.

The three warrant Offering Companies have issued warrants which have differing exercise levels, and differing conversion ratios and multiplying factors. Consequently, a purchaser of warrants must assess the risk/reward criteria of the available warrants, and make a selection based primarily on exercise level and time to expiry. The warrant chosen must also have reasonable volume, and buyer/seller quotes which are consistently close to one another.

The above discussion on delta and gearing may seem complex, and is not helped by the lack of standardisation by the Offering Companies. The simple thing to do is monitor the warrant prices, and work out the relative profits from time to time. These figures will show how the particular warrants are moving in response to moves in the index, and consequently which warrant to trade on the next signal.

TRADING THE GOLD INDEX

Table 22.2 shows that the warrant on the Gold Index has a high volatility of 50%, and that a fall of 70 points in the index resulted in a fall of 60¢ in the warrant price, giving a delta of 0.86. Chapter 18 showed that an upward move of 105 points in the Gold Index resulted in a rise of 83¢ in the warrant price, giving a delta of 0.79.

Figure 21.1 shows that on 23/3/98 there were no trades in the Gold Index warrant, and the buyer/seller quote was 2.45/2.65. Consequently, if we particularly wanted to buy on this day we may have to pay $2.65, even though the fair price may be only $2.55.

The Gold Index warrants look promising as a trading tool, but because they are not actively traded and have wide buyer/seller quotes, the actual profits obtained may be less than theoretically anticipated.

INDEX WARRANT SENSITIVITY TO INPUT PARAMETERS

There are five input parameters or factors to the BSOPM which influence the price of a warrant. The warrant price sensitivity to these factors is discussed fully in *Trading Stock Options and Warrants*, so only a brief comment is given here.

Volatility

Of the five input parameters, changes to volatility produce the largest changes in warrant price.

This can be demonstrated by taking the worked example at the start of this chapter for the Macquarie call warrant, and changing the volatility values. With a volatility of 31% the warrant price is $4.50. Corresponding warrant prices with a range of volatilities are listed below.

Volatility (%)	27	29	31	33	35
Warrant price ($)	4.21	4.35	4.50	4.62	4.76

When the All Ordinaries Index makes regular daily moves of 30 to 40 points, its volatility is higher than those times when the daily moves are, say, 20 to 30 points. This volatility is reflected in the price of the warrants.

Time to Expiry

The time to expiry affects the warrant time premium, which in turn affects the warrant price, because the warrant price is the sum of the intrinsic value plus the time premium. This time premium falls uniformly as the time to expiry decreases, though in the last four weeks to expiry the fall in price quickens. This behaviour is shown in Figure 22.1 for the same Macquarie call warrant used above (see page 143). We assume all the other BSOPM input factors remain constant while the time is decreasing.

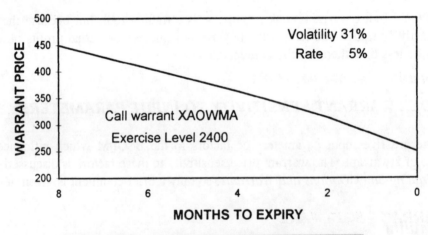

FIGURE 22.1 Warrant Price vs Time To Expiry

Notice that for this warrant with its conversion ratio of 1:1 and multiplying factor of 0.01, the value at expiry is $2.56.

The value is obtained as:

Intrinsic value = (2656 – 2400) × 0.01 = $2.56

150

Index Value and Exercise Level

The numeric values of the index value and exercise level determine whether the warrant is out-of-the-money, at-the-money or in-the-money. This in turn affects the magnitude of the warrant price change for a change in the index value. In other words, the warrant delta is dependent upon this relationship. As a rule of thumb, in-the-money warrants have a higher delta than at-the-money warrants, which have a higher delta than out-of-the-money warrants, all other factors being equal.

This result is seen in Table 22.2, by comparing the 123 point delta values for warrants of a particular offering company. The three DB call warrants have exercise levels of 2800, 3000 and 3200 with corresponding 123 point deltas of 16¢, 11¢ and 7¢ respectively. Similarly, for the two Macquarie put warrants with index levels of 2600 and 2200, the corresponding 123 point deltas are -77¢ and -51¢ respectively.

Risk-less Interest Rate

The current risk-free interest rate (e.g. the 90 day bill rate) has a minor effect upon the warrant price, with higher/lower interest rates producing slightly higher/lower warrant prices.

Sensitivity to Market Mood

The market mood has an effect on the warrant price, and in a rising market a call warrant will command a higher premium than in a flat market. This increase in warrant price is to be expected, as the market is factoring in an increase in the future volatility of the index.

WARRANT SOFTWARE

Software to calculate warrant and option prices is readily available from a number of suppliers. This software may be a single program, or it may be a part of a much larger charting and analysis package.

The warrant prices in this book have been calculated using the BSOPM contained in the QuickOptions module from the larger Omega Research SuperCharts 4 package. Details of software suppliers are given in Chapter 31.

Chapter 23

INVESTMENT COMPANIES & INDEX-LINKED PRODUCTS

PREVIOUS CHAPTERS HAVE suggested ways of picking the medium-term market trends, and trading these trends using appropriate financial products. So far only index warrants have been discussed because we can trade both the uptrends and downtrends using the All Ordinaries Index warrants.

In this chapter we turn our attention to other tradeable financial products which have less risk than warrants, but which can give very acceptable returns. Most of these products are suitable for buying on uptrends, and then converting to a cashed-up position at the start of downtrends.

Chapter 25 discusses short selling of equities which can be a profitable strategy in falling markets. Short selling is permissible on the ASX, but mainly practised by professional traders.

The Over 50s are particularly aware of managed funds, as this is the most popular area for investing superannuation money and other monies for the long haul. The term "managed funds" has various connotations, and is used in the literature to encompass managed investments, investment funds, unit trusts, mutual funds, etc. where a manager is paid to look after the investment – see *The Over 50s Investor* by Desmond Connelly.

Managed funds invest in the major areas of cash, fixed interest, equities (shares) and property, with a further partitioning into Australian and international holdings, and in the case of equities a partitioning into income or growth.

A particular managed fund will invest in a specific selection of one or more of these areas, so fund A may be heavily weighted in cash, for example, while fund

B may be heavily weighted in Australian growth equities. Brokers and fund managers publish the relative performance of the various areas of investment, and the different areas wax and wane in their returns on a year-by-year basis. However, over a 5-to-10-year period the growth and dividend return from quality equities outperforms the other areas of investment.

Even so, there is a disquieting statistic which shows about 68% of Australian retail equity trusts, with histories greater than five years, have under-performed the All Ordinaries Accumulation Index over the five years to September 1997. One reason for this under-performance is entry fees of typically 2% and annual management fees of a further 2%.

Consequently, there is a growing trend to invest in indexed funds which give investors direct access to financial products that perform in accordance with particular stock accumulation indices, and have lower fees than the traditional managed funds.

Top US investor, Warren Buffet of Berkshire Hathaway fame, wrote in the 1996 annual report that:

> "the best way to own common stocks is through an index fund which charges minimal fees. Those following in this path are sure to beat the net results (after fees and expenses) of the great majority of investment professionals."

On the Australian scene there are a variety of ways to implement this advice. One method is to purchase companies on the ASX which are either investment companies or are index-linked companies. An alternative method is to invest in managed funds which are specifically index-linked. Each approach is discussed below, along with trading strategies applicable to each.

If we trade investment companies listed on the ASX, then normal rates of brokerage apply on buying and selling, as discussed in Chapter 21. Alternatively, to invest in managed funds an entry or exit fee may be applicable, along with an annual management fee. These fees vary from fund to fund, and some are listed below. Some brokers and financial planners will rebate all, or part, of these fees.

The goal of this trading or investing is for our portfolio to grow at a faster rate than inflation, and preferably at a higher rate than the benchmark All Ordinaries Accumulation Index. For the 10 years to June 1997 the All Ordinaries Accumulation Index grew at a compounded rate of 9.1% p.a., while the CPI compounded at 3.9% p.a.

INVESTMENT COMPANIES

There are several investment companies listed on the ASX, with Australian Foundation Investment Company (AFIC) and Argo Investments being the two largest and most popular. Both companies have been in existence for over 50 years, and have build up a core portfolio of quality Australian stocks for growth and dividends. In addition to the core stocks, the companies are continually researching smaller companies with good management and prospects for earnings growth in the medium to longer term.

Investment companies have holdings in many other companies, but do not weight their portfolios to replicate the AOI. The investment companies' growth comes from the performance of their own researched portfolio. Dividends are paid to their shareholders from the portfolio income.

The better investment companies like AFIC and Argo out-perform the All Ordinaries Accumulation Index, though they too can have some lean years. Sooner or later investors come to realise that soundly run investment companies should be a part of their long-term portfolio.

Australian Foundation Investment Company

AFIC's goal is to consistently generate growth and returns above the All Ordinaries Accumulation Index, through investing in selected Australian equities. Investments are chosen for their profitability and long-term growth prospects, and are monitored by a board of directors drawn from captains of industry, most of whom are also directors of other top Australian companies.

AFIC is the largest investment company listed on the ASX, and at June 1997 had a portfolio valued at $1.46 billion. There were 44,000 shareholders and 2,900 holders of convertible notes. Administrative expenses for 1996/97 were less than 0.2%.

For the ten years to July 1997 AFIC made a total of seven bonus or rights issues. An investment of $1,000 in AFIC in June 1987 grew to just over $4,000 by June 1997, provided all bonus and rights issues and dividends were reinvested in the company. This represents a compound growth rate of 15.3% p.a., while the All Ordinaries Accumulation Index return was 9.1% p.a. and the CPI was 3.9% p.a. AFIC dividends grew at an annual rate of 10.5%, adjusted for bonus issues.

Bonus issues do not in themselves increase the value of a shareholding, but provided the dividend per share is maintained after the bonus, an increased return accrues from the higher number of shares held. It is common for share prices to fall on the announcement of a bonus, then gradually rise again to the pre-bonus levels. Similarly, rights issues increase the number of shares, but also provide new working capital for the company.

AFIC has a dividend reinvestment plan where dividends can be reinvested at a 5% discount to market price.

Figure 23.1 shows a monthly chart of AFIC for the 10 years from 1988 to 1998, corrected for bonus and rights issues. The chart is drawn with a semi-log scale. This chart is "similar but different" to the chart for AOI shown in Figure 3.1, but shows that AFIC moves in step with the AOI. Because AFIC makes frequent bonus and rights issues, it is necessary that its price chart be updated to take this into account, as an uncorrected chart gives a false picture of AFIC's performance.

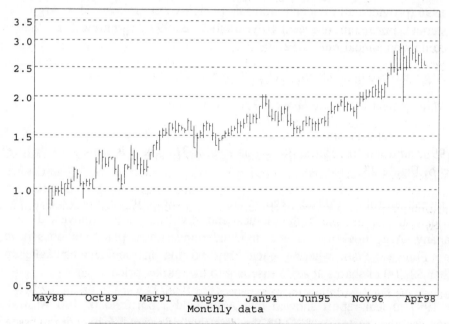

FIGURE 23.1 Monthly AFIC Over 10 Years

Companies like AFIC trade above and below their net asset backing depending on the mood of the market. This net asset value is provided by the company each month. At 28/2/98 the asset backing was $2.50, with a post-tax asset backing of $2.24, while the shares closed on 27/2/98 at $2.62. Investment companies provide pre-tax and post-tax valuations. Post-tax covers the situation of the company quitting all its investments at market value at that date, and consequently paying tax on accrued profits and capital gains, before a distribution of net assets to shareholders.

The AFIC office phone number is (03) 9650 9911, while details of AFIC's performance and current net asset value are available on 1800 780 784, or on the Internet at http://www.afi.com.au

Argo Investments

Argo celebrated its 50th anniversary in 1996 with a list of achievements:

- The annual net asset backing for the year to March 1988 (that took in the market crash of October 1987) resulted in an overall decline from $2.65 to $2.54.

- Argo has made 40 cash and bonus issues since 1950.

- An investment in Argo compounded at 20.5% p.a. for the 20 years to June 1996 (provided all dividends and sale of rights were reinvested in Argo shares). For the more recent 10 years to June 1997 Argo grew at a compound annual rate of 12.3%.

- Argo had group assets of $744 million and 22,000 shareholders.

- Management fees were about 0.3% of net assets p.a.

Figure 23.2 opposite shows a monthly chart of Argo for the 10 years from 1988 to 1998, adjusted for bonus and rights issues. The chart is similar to the AFIC chart of Figure 23.1.

An investment of $1,000 in Argo in June 1987 grew to $3,200 by June 1997, provided all bonus and rights issues and dividends were reinvested in the company. Argo does not have a dividend reinvestment plan, but does have a Share Purchase Plan, whereby each May existing shareholders can take up a further $2,500 of shares at a 5% discount to the market price.

The 1997 annual report showed that Argo held a portfolio of 190 Australian companies and trusts. At 28/2/98 the asset backing was $3.40, with a post-tax asset backing of $3.05, while the shares closed on 27/2/98 at $3.70.

Details of Argo's performance are available on (08) 8212 2055 or (02) 9221 1600.

A point to note about AFIC and Argo are the steep falls which both suffered in the mini-crash of October 1997. Admittedly, an investor would need to be very quick in buying on this one-day hiccup, but times of excessive pessimism present buying opportunities for AFIC and Argo, as they hold portfolios of quality stocks which participate in any recovery.

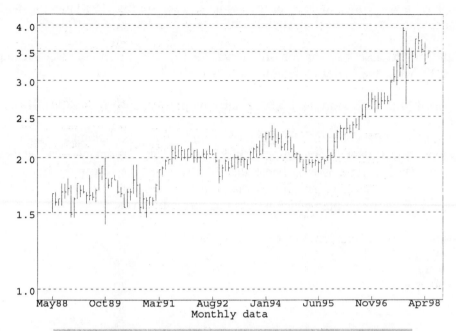

FIGURE 23.2 Monthly Argo Investments Over 10 Years

Milton Corporation

Milton Corporation is a smaller investment company with assets of around $360 million at June 1997 invested in a portfolio comprising 141 selected Australian companies.

Milton also rewards shareholders with bonus issues and rights issues at a discount, and for the 12 years to July 1997 Milton made a total of 15 bonus or rights issues. An investment of $1,000 in Milton in June 1987 grew to just over $3,800 by June 1997, provided all bonus and rights issues and dividends were reinvested in the company. This represents a compound growth rate of 14.5% p.a.

Administration costs were less than 0.35% of total assets for 1997. Figure 23.3 overleaf shows a monthly chart of Milton over 10 years from 1988 to 1998, adjusted for bonuses and rights issues. The chart for Milton is seen to be similar to AFIC and Argo, and during the past three years the share price of each company has doubled.

A comparison of the cumulative annual returns for each of the three investment companies over the past 10 years, as published in their June 1997 annual reports, gives AFIC 15.3%, Argo 12.3% and Milton 14.5%. Thus each investment company gives comparable returns, with the variations being due to each company's managers selecting slightly different stocks for their portfolios.

At 28/2/98 the asset backing for Milton was $9.15, with a post-tax asset backing of $8.32, while the shares closed on 27/2/98 at $9.00.

Details of Milton's performance are available on (02) 9233 4166 or 1800 641 024.

Milton is part of a stable of investment companies with cross holdings comprising Chatham Investment Company, Milkirk Investment Company and Matine Limited. During 1998 it is possible that Milton will take direct ownership of these three companies, and should this happen, then introduce a discounted dividend reinvestment plan which it does not currently have.

Postscript: This rationalisation took place on 30/6/98.

FIGURE 23.3   Monthly Milton Corp Over 10 Years

AMP

AMP floated in June 1998, and will be a stock of great interest to traders and investors. AMP is classified as an insurance company, though it does have about half its $8 billion assets invested in equities, property and bonds.

Consequently AMP's share price will reflect overall market moves, and could offer an alternative way of trading the market trends, particularly through call and put warrants on AMP.

158

As well its own portfolio, AMP manages around $135 billion of investments, from which it earns management fees.

Postscript: AMP listed on 15/6/98 with a remarkable day's activity. From initial prices of $45.00 the stock closed at $23.00. Three weeks later the stock seems to be stabilising around the $20.00 level.

BANKERS TRUST LISTED COMPANIES

Bankers Trust (BT) has a number of listed property trusts. However, of more interest to us are its investment companies directed specifically at Australian equities, Australian resources and global equities which trade on the ASX.

These three companies allow an investor to proportion funds into areas of their choosing, and possibly select the entry and exit time from analysis of the AOI, All Industrials Index or the All Resources Index. Further, the three companies are often viewed as trading vehicles rather than for long-term investment. Each company has a dividend reinvestment plan, but not a share purchase plan. Management has a policy of trading the BT companies shares, and sometimes buy them when they are trading at a discount.

The BT management fees are about 1.4% p.a., which is higher than those for AFIC, Argo and Milton.

Details of the BT funds are available on 1800 023 336.

BT Australian Equities

The 1997 annual report for BT Australian Equities (BTE) states:

> "the Company's primary objective is the establishment of a portfolio of Australian shares which provide franked yield and growth for taxed Australian investors. The Company's medium to long-term goal is to exceed the return on the ASX All Industrials Accumulation Index and to provide a dividend yield higher than the average yield of those stocks comprised in the ASX All Industrials Accumulation Index."

In the ten years since inception in March 1987, BTE has achieved a pre-tax return of 18.7% p.a. (and a post-tax return of 13.9% p.a.) compared with 10.4% p.a. for the ASX All Industrials Accumulation Index.

At the time of the 1997 annual report BTE was holding a portfolio of 45 industrial stocks.

Figure 23.4 shows a monthly chart for BTE spanning 10 years, adjusted for any bonus and rights issues. This chart has a different pattern to that of the three previous investment companies.

Data in the BTE annual report shows the shares can trade at a premium or a discount to their net asset backing. During 1993 to 1997 the maximum discount has been about 9% and the maximum premium about 10%. This spread can lead to profitable trading strategies.

At 28/2/98 the asset backing was $0.74, while the shares closed on 27/2/98 at $0.74.

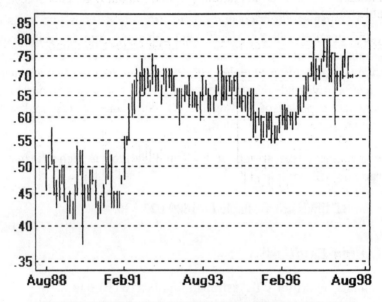

FIGURE 23.4   Monthly BT Equities Over 10 Years

BT Resources

The 1997 annual report for BT Resources (BTM) states:

> "the Company's principal objective is to achieve medium to long-term appreciation through investment in a portfolio of natural resource shares and to provide franked dividend income. The Company's medium to long-term goal is to exceed the return on the ASX All Resources Accumulation Index."

For the six years since inception in November 1991, BTM has achieved a pre-tax return of 5.3% p.a. (and a post-tax return of 4.7% p.a.) compared with 5.5% p.a. for the ASX All Resources Accumulation Index.

It is worth noting that in the 6 months to December 1997 the All Resources Accumulation Index fell 23.8% and BTM fell 24.7%, so BTM was replicating the index rather than out-performing it during this time.

At the time of the 1997 annual report BTE was holding a portfolio of 21 resource stocks. Figure 23.5 shows a monthly chart for BTM spanning the seven years since inception.

Data in the BTM annual report shows the shares can trade at a premium or a discount to their net asset backing. During 1993 to 1996 the maximum discount has been about 15% and the maximum premium about 6%. This spread can lead to profitable trading strategies.

At 28/2/98 the asset backing was $0.417, while the shares closed on 27/2/98 at $0.38.

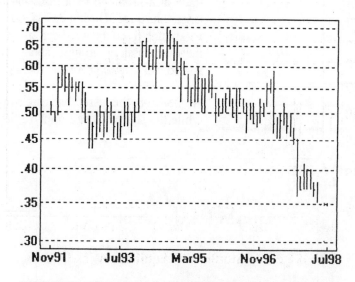

FIGURE 23.5 Monthly BT Resources Over 7 Years

BT Global

Most Australian global funds use the Morgan Stanley Capital International (MSCI) World Share Accumulation Index in $A as their benchmark. These funds hold shares in a selection of international companies, and move funds in and out of particular countries depending on the fund managers' assessment of risk and returns.

The 1997 annual report for BT Global (BTG) states:

> "the Company's principal objective is to achieve medium to long-term appreciation through investment in securities listed on the world's stock markets. The Company's medium to long-term goal is to exceed the return on the MSCI in $A."

For the 11 years since inception in October 1986, BTG has achieved a pre-tax return of 18.6% p.a. (and a post-tax return of 12.3%) compared with 11.0% p.a. for the MSCI Accumulation Index.

At the time of the 1997 annual report BTG was holding a portfolio spread over equities in several regions as:

North America	35.5%
Japan	16.0
Europe	15.7
Australia	13.5
Latin America	3.0
SE Asia	0.5
Liquid assets	11.0
Other assets	4.8
	100.0%

Figure 23.6 shows a monthly chart for BTG spanning 10 years, and takes into account any bonus and rights issues. Data in the BTG annual report shows the shares can trade at a premium or a discount to their net asset backing. During 1994 to 1997 the maximum discount has been about 20% and the maximum premium about 50%. This spread can lead to profitable trading strategies.

At 28/2/98 the asset backing was $0.761, while the shares closed on 27/2/98 at $0.64.

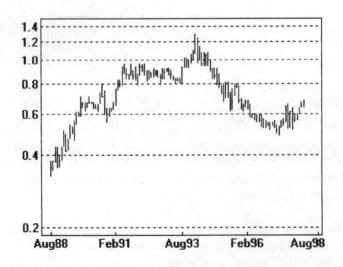

FIGURE 23.6 Monthly BT Global Over 10 Years

TEMPLETON GLOBAL GROWTH FUND

The December 1997 report of the Templeton Global Growth Fund (TGG) states that the principal activity of the Company is to invest in securities, consisting primarily of equity securities, listed on the world's stock exchanges. The Company seeks long-term appreciation from a globally diversified portfolio of investments.

The TGG managers have built a global portfolio of equities with an investment philosophy which emphasises "buying when others are despondently selling and selling when others are hungrily buying requires the greatest fortitude and pays the greatest potential rewards".

In turbulent times discounted stocks with long-term earnings potential are bought, to lay the foundation for future performance.

At December 1997 TGG held equities in 34 different countries, spread over several regions as:

North America	28.6%
Europe	47.5
Asia	10.4
Australasia	4.2
Latin America	6.9
Middle East/ Africa	2.4
	100.0%

Total portfolio value was about $117 million.

For the five years from December 1992 to December 1997 TGG achieved a pre-tax cumulative return of 16.9% p.a. (and a post-tax return of 15.0%) compared with 17.1% p.a. for the MSCI Accumulation Index. During that time the net asset backing grew from $1.25 to $2.14 on a pre-tax basis. Management fees are about 0.6% p.a.

TGG does not have a dividend reinvestment plan nor a share purchase plan. Figure 23.7 overleaf shows a monthly chart for TGG spanning 10 years. Once again, it is interesting to compare the price patterns between Figures 23.6 and 23.7. Both BTG and TGG are investors in global equities, but their share price performance is very different.

At 28/2/98 the asset backing was $1.88, while the shares closed on 27/2/98 at $1.74. Details of TGG are available on (03) 9866 4684.

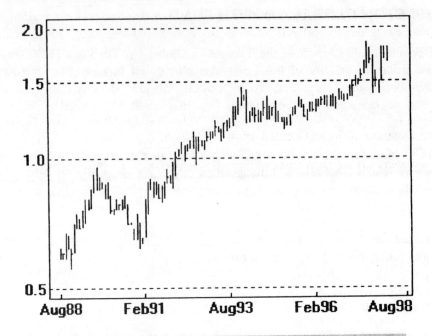

FIGURE 23.7   Monthly Templeton Global Over 10 Years

INDEX-LINKED PRODUCTS

The Benchmark Australian All Ordinaries Index Trust

The Benchmark Australian All Ordinaries Index Trust (BAT) commenced trading on the ASX in February 1997, and is a share investment fund which invests in a portfolio replicating the companies in the Australian AOI.

BAT's objective is to provide investment returns (before management fees) that match the performance of the All Ordinaries Accumulation Index.

BAT is similar to AFIC, Argo and Milton discussed above, in that it pays dividends from the dividends it receives. The prospectus estimates a dividend of about 3.4% p.a. This dividend needs be reinvested in BAT to achieve a compounding return akin to the All Ordinaries Accumulation Index, and BAT has a dividend reinvestment plan.

Management fees are estimated at about 0.5% p.a. plus a $6 quarterly fee per unitholder to cover registry and reports, etc.

Shares in BAT trade steadily, though usually in low volume, and there are some days with no trades. The BAT price follows the AOI value very closely with a 0.01 multiplier (i.e. AOI = 2574 points, BAT = $25.74). Figure 23.8 shows the BAT daily bar chart with volume in the lower trace, and the gaps represent days with no trades.

Details of BAT's performance are available from the Manager on (02) 9252 2688, or from Deutsche Morgan Grenfell on (02) 9256 1527.

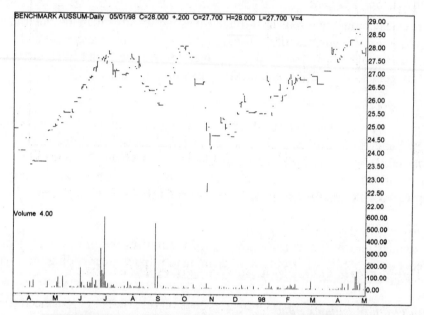

FIGURE 23.8   Daily Benchmark Australian AOI Trust

MANAGED FUNDS

There are scores of fund managers offering a range of managed funds to cater for individual tastes and preferences. The fund managers offer both superannuation and ordinary-type investments. Our particular interest is products with returns linked to the stock market indices.

Two such products having index-linked funds and a low fee structure are Barclays Global Investors and Bank Brussels Lambert (BBL) Funds Management Limited. Details of these products are included to give readers a feel for this type of fund, and are not intended as a recommendation or otherwise.

Barclays Investment Funds

The Barclays family of investment funds are listed below, with a brief description of the fund as defined by the fund manager. There are no entry or exit fees, but there is an entry/exit price spread which effectively amounts to a entry and exit fee. There is also an annual management fee. Barclays allow four switches a year between funds at no additional charge. Minimum initial investment is $1,000.

- *Diverse Stable Fund*

  Provides competitive returns through investing in Australian and international fixed interest securities, cash, listed property trusts and Australian and international shares. The fund is weighted towards cash and fixed interest. Management fee 1.25%, entry/exit spread 0.25% each way.

- *Diverse Growth Fund*

  Provides competitive returns through investing in Australian and international fixed interest securities, cash, listed property trusts and Australian and international shares. The fund is weighted towards Australian and international shares with growth potential. Management fee 1.25%, entry/exit spread 0.40% each way.

- *Australian Share Fund*

  Provides returns that consistently exceed the returns (before management fees) of the ASX All Ordinaries Accumulation Index over rolling three-year periods. Management fee 1.25%, entry/exit spread 0.55% each way.

- *All Ordinaries Index Fund*

  Provides returns that match (before management fees) the performance of the ASX All Ordinaries Accumulation Index. Management fee 0.95%, entry/exit spread 0.45% each way.

- *International Share Fund*

  Provides returns that consistently exceed the returns (before management fees) of the MSCI World Share Accumulation Index over rolling three-year periods. Management fee 1.25%, entry/exit spread 0.45% each way.

These funds are not traded on the ASX but can be purchased through the prospectus available from Barclays on 1800 222 743.

The All Ordinaries Index Fund is similar to BAT, as its objective is to provide investment returns (before management fees) that match the performance of the All Ordinaries Accumulation Index. This fund is due to commence in August 1998.

Postscript: The minimum initial investment in the Barclays Investment Funds has been raised to $50,000, while management fees are reduced to 0.65%.

BBL Investment Funds

The BBL family of investment funds are listed below, with a brief description of the fund as defined by the fund manager. There are no entry or exit fees, but there is an entry/exit price spread which effectively amounts to a entry and exit fee. There is also an annual management fee capped at 0.75%. BBL allow two switches a year between funds at no additional charge. Minimum initial investment in the BBL Investment Funds is $10,000.

- *The Director Industrial Leaders Fund*

  Provides returns similar to the ASX 100 Industrials Accumulation Index. Over a period of time the fund will become structured to replicate the equity weightings in the ASX 100 Industrials Index. Entry/exit spread 0.25% each way.

- *The Director Resource Leaders Fund*

  Provides returns similar to the ASX 100 Resources Accumulation Index. Over a period of time the fund will become structured to replicate the equity weightings in the ASX 100 Resources Index. Entry/exit spread 0.25% each way.

- *The Director Small Company Leaders Fund*

  Provides returns similar to the ASX Small Ordinaries Accumulation Index. The fund does not replicate the equity weightings in the ASX Small Ordinaries because of the large number of companies involved. Entry/exit spread 0.50% each way.

- *The Director Enhanced Yield Fund*

  Provides a return that is 0.5% to 1.0% p.a. greater than the total return on the SBCWDR Bank Bill Index measured over rolling 12-month periods. The fund manager stresses that there is some risk associated with this fund, and it can have negative returns because the market value of the bank bills fluctuate with variations in interest rates. Entry/exit spread 0.12% each way.

These funds are not traded on the ASX but can be purchased through the prospectus available from BBL on 1300 306 706.

PERSONAL INVESTMENT DIRECT ACCESS

At the start of this chapter it was noted that many brokers and financial planners will rebate all, or part, of the entry fees applicble to making investments in managed funds. One company rebating fees is Personal Investment Direct Access Pty Ltd (PIDA), which advertises regularly in the monthly magazines *Shares* and *Personal Investment*. This company gives no advice, but offers rebates on selected products of the following popular families of managed funds:

- Advance Asset Management Ltd

- BT Funds Management Ltd

- County Investment Management

- EquitiLink Australia Ltd

- JB Were Capital Markets Ltd

- Macquarie Investment Management Ltd

- MLC Investments Ltd

- National Mutual Asset Management Ltd

- Perpetual Funds Management

- Rothschild Australia Asset Management Ltd

Each of these managers have a family of funds drawn from Australian blue chip equities, Australian smaller companies, resource companies, overseas equities, property trusts, bonds, etc., somewhat akin to those discussed above in the Barclays and BBL Investment Funds. These funds are not strictly index-linked funds. However, they obviously do mirror the performance of the different stock market indices, in that if the All Industrials Index performs well, so too would the Australian blue chip equity funds.

Normal retail entry fees to these funds is typically 3% to 5%, though County Investment Management has no entry fee. PIDA rebates the entry fees such that net entry fee to the above funds is typically nil to 1%. PIDA receives an ongoing fee of up to 0.25% p.a. of funds invested.

The PIDA phone number is (03) 9603 3888.

Chapter 24

NEW SHARE FLOATS CAN BE WINNERS

WHEN CONSIDERING growth stocks to add to an investment portfolio, new floats should be considered carefully. New companies are being floated all the time, and in bullish times there can be a rush of new floats. Cold statistics show that investors in the majority of new floats do not do well, though there are always some gems amongst the duds.

However, there is one class of float that historically has done well, and that is the large public floats of companies which are household names and have a capitalisation above, say, $250 million. These particular floats are not spin-offs from parent companies, but are government corporations or privately-owned companies being floated to the public.

Table 24.1 overleaf lists the major new floats since 1991, which reads like a *Who's Who* of business. The companies float by issuing a prospectus with the invitation to take up shares at the issue price. Investors need be aware that a prospectus is a selling document, and independent advice from a stockbroker should be sought before taking up shares. Good floats are often over-subscribed, with investors being allocated fewer shares than they would like, so they top up through buying on the open market when the shares start trading.

Table 24.1 lists the issue price and the listing price – the latter being the close price on the first day of trading. Column 5 is the percentage gain between the issue price and the listing price, column 6 is the peak price to 31/3/98, column 7 is this peak expressed as a percentage from listing, and the last column is the closing price on 31/3/98.

TABLE 24.1 Major Floats Since 1991

Year	Company	Issue Price ($)	Listing Price ($)	Listing Gain (%)	Peak Price ($)	Peak Gain (%)	Price 31/3/98 ($)
1991	CBA	5.40	6.78	26	18.80	177	17.96
1992	WA Newspapers	1.00	1.55	55	6.74	335	5.63
1992	Fairfax	1.20	1.52	27	3.53	132	2.89
1992	GIO	2.40	2.49	4	4.75	91	4.55
1993	Woolworths	2.45	2.60	6	6.24	140	5.65
1993	Seven Network	2.00	2.72	36	6.26	130	5.55
1993	Elders Australia	1.00	1.25	25	**	91	0.66
1994	Crown Casino	1.20	1.60	33	3.06	91	0.66
1994	SGIO	1.00	1.17	17	1.70	45	1.47
1994	CSL	2.40	2.40	0	11.95	398	11.18
1994	Davids	1.65	1.54	-7	1.94	26	1.05
1994	Tabcorp	2.25	2.24	0	8.28	270	8.10
1994	Acacia	2.00	2.98	49	3.46	16	2.04
1995	Sydney Casino	1.28	1.44	12	2.45	70	1.19
1995	Qantas	1.90	2.32	22	3.21	38	2.47
1995	Lihir	1.50	1.87	25	2.59	38	1.98
1995	David Jones	2.00	2.08	4	2.08	0	1.75
1996	Bank West	2.05	2.52	23	3.32	32	3.14
1996	CBA Instal't Receipts	6.00	6.08	1	##		17.96
1996	National Mutual	1.50	1.75	17	3.66	109	3.29
1996	Orogen	1.70	2.05	21	4.15	102	3.08
1996	Infrastr. Trust of Aust.	1.00	1.33	33	1.55	17	1.35
1997	Colonial Ltd	2.60	3.25	25	5.25	62	4.95
1997	Adsteam Marine	2.00	2.71	35	3.38	25	3.04
1997	Telstra Instal't Receipts	1.95	2.67	36	4.00	50	3.89

** Elders taken over by Futuris in March 1997 at about $2.23
CBA Instalment Receipts had a second payment of $4.45 to become fully paid

The last column of Table 24.1 shows the closing prices on 31/3/98. Compared with the listing price in column 4, it is seen that only five of the 25 stocks are below their listing price. There are typically three or four major floats a year, and the average gain on listing is about 20%. Brokers Hogan & Partners, JB Were and others put out data on these new floats which show the average annualised return from the listing price is above 20% (not including dividend returns).

Table 24.1 demonstrates that it is worthwhile applying for shares in major new floats, and if unsuccessful there, then buying those shares in the first few days of trading.

The Intelligent Investor's Guide To Share Buying (4th Edition) by Tim Hewat contains an informative Appendix, "Finding Merit in Floats", contributed by Herb Qualls.

A word of caution. We should not be carried away by the euphoria created by the success of the Telstra float, and think that the only companies which achieve spectacular gains are major new floats. This is not so. There are scores of examples of long-established companies which have achieved similar or better returns over the past few years, e.g. AGL, Brambles, Lend Lease, the major banks (from their nadir in 1993), etc.

Part of the attraction of major new floats is that we can have two bites at the cherry. Firstly, there can be an immediate share price rise on listing. Secondly, as the company begins operating in its new identity, and develops a track record of profits and efficiency, its value may gradually increase.

EQUITY WARRANTS ON NEW FLOATS

Equity warrants on stocks are very popular, so the warrant offering companies quickly make warrants available on the major new share floats. The two most recent floats that have equity warrants are Colonial and Telstra.

Colonial started trading in May 1997 at around $3.30. The first equity call warrant issued was CGHWSA, having a strike price of $3.50 and expiry 26/11/98. The warrant began trading on 18/7/97, and that day Colonial closed at $3.48 with the warrant at 52¢. Up to 31/3/98 the peak values of Colonial and the warrant are $5.25 and $1.81 respectively. The percentage returns are shown in Table 24.2 overleaf.

Telstra began trading on 17/11/97 in the form of Instalment Receipts (Telstra IRS) and closed at $2.67. Several equity call warrants began trading on the same day. The warrant TLSWDA has a strike price of $2.50 and expiry 16/10/98, and closed the first day at 56¢. Up to 31/3/98 the peak values of Telstra IRS and the warrant are $4.00 and $1.58 respectively. The percentage returns are shown in Table 24.2.

TABLE 24.2 Return On Colonial And Telstra vs Warrants

Share	First Date	Price (¢)	Peak Price (¢)	Gain (%)
Colonial	18/7/97	348	525	51
CGHWSA	18/7/97	52	181	248
Telstra IRS	17/11/97	267	400	50
TLIWDA	17/11/97	56	158	182

It is common for equity warrants with time to expiry of greater than say nine months, to have a gearing of typically three times, i.e. the percentage change in the price of the warrant is about three times the percentage change in the price of the underlying share.

Part IV

CLOSING TOPICS

Chapter 25

SHORT SELLING

"SHORT SELLING" IS the term applied to selling shares we do not own and buying them back sometime in the future. If the shares have gone down in price we make a profit, but if they have increased, a loss is made on buying them back.

Short selling is popular on the NYSE, and has its supporters, but also its detractors.

For many years short selling was banned on the ASX due to an abuse of the system, such as occasions where more stock was shorted than was on issue, and situations where the outstanding stock was held by a "corner" who asked exorbitant prices for the stock. In recent years short selling has been reintroduced with strict rules laid down by the ASX.

In principle, selling short in a falling market is no different to buying long in a rising market, as we are trying to profit from the direction of the market trend. Short selling has always been an integral part of the options market, as the writer of options often does not own that stock (see *Trading Stock Options and Warrants*).

ASX RULES ON SHORT SELLING

Copies of the rules on short selling are available from the ASX. Not all stocks may be sold short, and the ASX issues a list of Approved Securities which changes from time to time. At March 1998 there were 223 stocks on the approved list of shares which could be shorted.

Some basic rules on short selling on the ASX are:

- The stock must have more than 50 million shares issued.

- The stock must have a capitalisation greater than $100 million.

- The ASX must be satisfied with the level of the stock's liquidity.

- Not more than 10% of the issued number of shares in an Approved Security may be sold short.

- The short sale must not be transacted at a price lower than the previous sale.

BROKERS REQUIREMENTS FOR SHORT SELLING

A seller must inform the broker in advance that the order is to sell short. The broker must confirm that the stock is on the Approved Security list, and the number of shares to be sold does not breach the 10% limit. After the transaction is executed it is tagged on the market as a short sale by using the letter S, and also on the seller's contract note.

Before executing a short sale, deposits of at least 20% of the value of the transaction are required by the broker. This deposit can be in cash or equities, and may need to be topped up if the price of the sold shares rises, or the value of the deposited equities falls.

If the value of the sold shares rises the short seller faces a loss. To protect all parties in such a case, the broker is empowered to cover the transaction (buy back the shares) if margin calls are not met promptly.

It is apparent that the mechanics of short selling a stock are more complex than buying a stock, because scrip still has to be delivered to the purchaser. This scrip has to be borrowed through the broker, which incurs a fee to the lender, along with a monitoring and maintenance fee to the broker.

Individual brokers have different rules for deposits on short selling, additional to the ASX rules. Some brokers such as Green Line will not take such an order, while others do.

Hogan & Partners have an upper limit of $75,000 transaction value per trade, and require a 40% deposit. Normal brokerage fees apply to buying and selling, plus a $30 establishment fee and a $3 per day maintenance fee.

Those interested in short selling need to discuss the various rules and requirements with their broker well in advance of placing any orders.

WHY BOTHER WITH SHORT SELLING?

Short selling may sound too hard, but the attraction is that markets fall more quickly than they rise. The choices available for trading in a falling market are:

- Stand aside till the market turns up.

- Buy put warrants.

- Write call options.

- Short sell stocks.

- Sell Share Price Index (SPI) futures. The SPI is popular with professional traders, and is discussed in *Understanding Futures Trading in Australia* by Christopher Tate.

As an example of the costs involved in short selling, suppose NAB is trading at $20 and we short sell 500 shares through Hogan & Partners. The transaction value is $500 \times 20 = \$10,000$ and is below the $75,000 upper limit. The deposit required is $10,000 \times 0.4 = \$4,000$. Transaction costs are:

Selling brokerage at say 1.5%	$150
Short sell establishment fee	30
If hold trade 6 weeks (or 42 days @ $3 per day)	126
Buy back brokerage, say	150
Total fees	**456**

Thus, in this example to break even on the trade NAB needs to fall $\frac{456}{500} = \$0.91$ to $19.09.

If NAB falls $2.00 over the six weeks of the trade then the net profit is $500 \times 2.00 - 456 = \$544$. This represents a return on the $4,000 deposit of 13% over the six-week period.

177

Chapter 26

RISK AND MONEY MANAGEMENT

TRADING IS A business, and needs to be treated as a business. Great care must be taken to look after its major asset – the capital. The management of risk needs to be carefully thought out and adhered to.

Technical indicators may start the journey, but risk and money management help get us safely to our destination. Some elements of risk and money management are:

- Risk per trade.

- Allocation per trade.

- Risk/reward ratio.

- Account drawdown.

Warren Buffet says that building up wealth has more to do with controlling losses than making profits. Larry Hite of Mint Investment Management Company says to never risk more than 1% of total capital on any trade. Ed Seykota of *Market Wizards* limits his risk to 5% of capital on any trade. Other writers and wizards have risk limits somewhere between the 1% and 5% values, and Daryl Guppy recommends 2%. What is important is to determine a risk figure and to understand its implications to each trade. Then it is imperative to be disciplined, and ruthless, in accepting losses as they occur during the course of trading.

The percentage values chosen for allocation and risk are for the individual to chose. Traders with large accounts can afford to operate with low values of risk

(1% of a $1 million account is $10,000). Smaller traders have to accept larger risk values in setting realistic loss limits.

Suppose we have a total portfolio of $100,000 with $20,000 allocated to trading. If we use a 2% limit, then 2% of the trading kitty is $400.

A commonly used risk/reward ratio is 2:1, which means that if the average loss per trade is $400, then the average profit must be $800 or more on the good trades.

A system with these parameters can be profitable if it is right 50% of the time. Very simply, over 20 typical trades 10 will give a profit of $10 \times 800 = \$8,000$ and 10 trades will give a loss of $10 \times 400 = \$4,000$, resulting in an overall profit of $4,000 (before brokerage and stamp duty). However, with any system there can be a string of consecutive loss trades, and a system that is right 50% of the time may give five consecutive losses equating to a cumulative loss in this example of $2,000.

"Account drawdown" is the term used to describe the amount the trading account goes against us on an annual basis. The rule of thumb is that the annual percentage return from a system is about three times the account drawdown. Thus, to achieve a return of 30% p.a. we must anticipate an account drawdown of say 10% sometime during the year. With a starting kitty of $20,000 a 10% drawdown is $2,000.

Trading a kitty of $20,000 and applying the 2% risk rule, a straight stock transaction works as follows:

	Credit ($)	Debit ($)
Purchase 200 BAT at $19.75 (including $50 brokerage)		4,000
Sell 200 BAT at $18.25 (including $50 brokerage)	3,600	
Loss on trade		**400**

The loss represents 2% of the trading kitty but 10% of the capital allocated to the trade.

The allocation per trade needs to be considered, as it too is an important parameter in the trading system. With a trading kitty of $20,000 it may be prudent to limit any one trade to, say, a maximum of $4,000. The trade-off between risk and allocation needs to be addressed before entering a trade, as discussed below.

Our trading strategy involves trading index-linked funds as well as warrants which are geared to the underlying indices. Thus to stipulate a percentage figure for risk management, it is necessary to look at some typical price moves in the indices, and find the corresponding price moves in the index-linked funds and warrants.

TYPICAL PROFITS AND LOSSES

Chapter 16 shows that the MACD indicator with profit stops applied to weekly AOI gives 12 winning trades for an average profit of 10.7%, and 11 loss trades for an average loss of -3.7%.

With a trading kitty of $20,000 it is prudent to allocate at least $3,000 per trade. With a fixed brokerage fee of $50 for buying and for selling, the break-even point on a $3,000 trade is a rise of 3.3%, i.e. the profit is $3000 \times 0.033 = \$100$ which just balances the $100 brokerage.

Trading BAT

Suppose we buy $3,000 worth of BAT on a MACD up signal but it turns out to be a loss trade. The AOI will move typically -3.7% before the next MACD signal to quit the trade. As the BAT has a gearing of one times AOI, then the BAT price will move against us 3.7%, corresponding to a dollar loss of $3000 \times 0.037 = \$111$. Including brokerage of $100, the gross loss is $210, which corresponds to 1.1% of the trading kitty.

In a typical profit trade BAT will gain 10.7%. The return becomes $3000 \times 0.107 = \$321$ less brokerage for a net profit of $220, corresponding to 1.1% of the trading kitty.

The ratio of average percentage profit to average percentage loss is $\frac{1.1}{1.1} = 1.0$, which will not generate a profit with a system which is right 50% of the time. Brokerage has eroded the theoretical profit ratio from $\frac{10.7}{3.7} = 2.9$ to just 1.0.

Trading AOI Warrants

Suppose we buy $3,000 worth of AOI index warrants (either call or put) on a MACD signal but it turns out to be a loss trade. The AOI will move typically -3.7% before the next MACD signal to quit the trade. As the warrants have a gearing of around three times the AOI, then the warrant price will move against us $3 \times 3.7 = 11.1\%$, which corresponds to a dollar loss of $3000 \times 0.111 = \$333$. Including brokerage of $100, the gross loss is say $430, corresponding to 2.2% of trading kitty.

In a typical profit trade the AOI will gain 10.7%. The warrant price will move typically $3 \times 10.7 = 32.1\%$, and the return becomes $3000 \times 0.321 = \$963$ less brokerage for a net profit of $860, corresponding to 4.3% of trading kitty.

The ratio of average percentage profit to average percentage loss is now $\frac{4.3}{2.2} = 2.0$, which could generate a profit with a system which is right 50% of the time. Brokerage in this case has eroded the theoretical profit ratio from 2.9 to 2.0.

Trading BAT Using Technical Stops

Chapter 6 briefly touched on technical stops as a method to control losses. The method is practical and logical, and involves the following steps:

1. For a given trade, specify the maximum allowable loss, and the maximum allocation of capital for the trade.

2. Determine the buy price.

3. Determine the stop-loss price.

4. Calculate the maximum acceptable loss per share.

5. Calculate the number of shares to buy.

6. Check that the cost of the shares is within the allocation limits.

Once again, suppose we are trading a kitty of $20,000 with a 2% risk rule, equating to a maximum loss of $400 per trade. Allowing for total brokerage of $100 on the trade, then $300 is the maximum loss we can accept on the shares or warrants themselves. In this example, the maximum allocation per trade is $5,000.

Suppose the AOI is in a trading range between 2400 points and 2450 points, as shown in Figure 26.1. The price moves to 2470 points, which we assume triggers a buy on the MACD, or whichever indicators we are using. We reason that if the trade is a whipsaw, a break below, say, 2380 points will confirm the reversal. Thus the technical stop is set at this level.

In order to participate in this trade, we decide on the BAT as the trading vehicle. Thus we will buy BAT shares at $24.70, and place a stop to quit if BAT falls to $23.80. The loss per share if the trade goes sour is $24.70 - 23.80 = \$0.90$.

The maximum loss we can accept on the shares themselves is $300. Consequently, the maximum number of shares to buy is $\frac{300}{0.90} = 333$, and these will cost $333 \times 24.70 = \$8,225$.

As $8,225 is above the allocation limit of $5,000, we would scale down the purchase to $\frac{5000}{24.70} =$ say 200 BAT shares, thereby also reducing the maximum loss that might have to be taken. Note that the stop level remains fixed, and is not relaxed to allow the full $300 loss.

If the AOI rises by 10.7%, then BAT will rise by $24.70 \times 0.107 = \$2.64$. The gross profit on the trade is $200 \times 2.64 = \$528$, for a net profit after brokerage of $428.

Working through this example may seem tedious and mathematical. Successful trading is serious stuff. If it is treated with a "She'll be right mate" cavalier attitude, then it is only a matter of time before the kitty is wiped out.

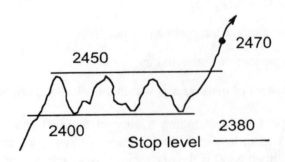

FIGURE 26.1 Application Of Technical Trading Stops

LARGER TRADES

We could choose a trading strategy which trades only index warrants on the AOI and the Gold Index, and trade a $20,000 kitty in two parcels of $10,000.

For a $10,000 trade of AOI index warrants, brokerage is still about $100 total. A typical 3.7% loss trade translates to a net loss of $10000 \times 3 \times 0.037 + 100 = $1,210 or 6.0% of the trading kitty (assuming a warrant gearing of 3 times).

Similarly, a typical 10.7% profit trade translates to a net gain of $10000 \times 3 \times 0.107 - 100 = $3,110 or 15.5% of the trading kitty.

For the $10,000 AOI warrant trade the ratio of average percentage profit to average percentage loss is $\frac{15.5}{6.0} = 2.6\%$, whereas for the $3,000 trade the ratio is lower at 2.0%.

NOTE: Trading half the kitty in a single trade breaks all the rules (other than maximising profits). The typical loss is shown above to be $1,210, or 6.0% of trading kitty, and is way above the sensible limit of 2.0%.

Chapter 27

PORTFOLIO PROTECTION WITH INDEX PUT WARRANTS

AT APRIL 1998 the index warrants have been trading for 3.5 months, and the AOI put warrants have proved to be the most popular. During this time the market has been going up, so the put warrants have not been bought so much to trade, but rather as a hedge for investors with share portfolios.

If we hold a share portfolio which we do not want to sell, but we are anticipating a fall in the market, then one way of cushioning the fall in the portfolio is to buy AOI put warrants which will appreciate in value if the market falls.

As an example, suppose the AOI is around 2850 points and we expect the market to fall during the next few weeks. We decide to buy AOI put warrants, and look for one which is just out-of-the-market. The Macquarie put warrant XAOWMQ is ideal, as it has exercise level of 2600 points (see Table 22.2). Further, it is a popular warrant and has considerable turnover each day.

In late April the uptrend in the AOI was punctuated by a four-day retreat. The relevant closing levels for the AOI and the put warrant XAOWMQ are listed in Table 27.1 opposite.

Table 27.1 shows that from 23/4/98 to 29/4/98 the AOI fell from 2877 points to 2749 points. This represents a fall of 128 points or 4.4%. Over the same time the put warrant XAOWMQ rose from $1.18 to $1.55 (i.e. $0.37), for a gain of 31% and representing a gearing of $\frac{31}{4.4} = 7.0$.

For want of better data from a longer downtrend, these values to can be used to work through the calculations to determine how many warrants to buy for a given level of portfolio protection.

Suppose the share portfolio is valued at $50,000 with the AOI around 2850 points. If the AOI falls 4.4%, the portfolio will fall about the same percentage for a paper loss of $50000 \times 0.044 =$ $2,200.

The number of XAOWMQ warrants that need be purchased to fully cover the portfolio fall in value is $\frac{2200}{0.37} = 5946$ which would cost $5946 \times 1.18 =$ $7,016. Thus in this case, buying a $7,016 parcel of put warrants and selling them after the 4.4% fall in the AOI maintains the overall value of the portfolio.

TABLE 27.1 Values Of All Ordinaries Index And Put Warrant

Date	AOI (Points)	XAOWMQ ($)
22/4/98	2856	1.25
23/4/98	2877	1.18
24/4/98	2854	1.26
27/4/98	2818	1.33
28/4/98	2781	1.43
29/4/98	2749	1.55
30/4/98	2762	1.50

Chapter 22 shows that different warrants have different gearing, being dependent upon index level, warrant exercise level and time to expiry. Thus, before purchasing put warrants to protect a portfolio, the gearing of the available warrants should be checked.

DOWNSIDE

The above example shows that put warrants are effective in protecting a share portfolio against market falls. However, as in all trades, there is the possibility that the market will turn against us. If the market turns upward, our portfolio may show paper profits, but the warrant trade will need to be closed out for a real loss.

Once the put warrant trade is opened, the trade should be treated as any other trade. Thus, it could be closed on the weekly MACD profit target stop rules. Alternatively, it could have a stop level calculated to close the trade if the market turns upwards.

Buying AOI put warrants is a valid strategy to protect a share portfolio, but there is little point in buying put warrants for this purpose unless we are confident the market has moved into a downtrend. As discussed in Chapter 22, the price of a warrant comprises intrinsic value and time premium, with the time premium reducing to zero at the warrant expiry time. Thus, even if the AOI value remains steady the value of our put warrants will still fall.

Chapter 28

TRADING STRATEGIES FOR INVESTMENT COMPANIES & INDEX-LINKED PRODUCTS

DIFFERENT STRATEGIES can be adopted for trading index warrants, investment companies and index-linked funds.

Firstly, we need a method of determining the market trend. Secondly, we need to decide what level of risk we are prepared to accept, as this dictates which financial product to trade. We also need to consider how much time we are prepared to devote each week to market analysis and monitoring, and how many indicators to use for confirmation of trends.

DETERMINING THE TREND

Part I has investigated a variety of technical indicators for finding the medium-term and long-term trends in the Australian stock market, with the preferred method being MACD on weekly data, and using stops to exit trades before the MACD exit signal is given.

Confirmation of the trend can be obtained from a variety of indicators including the Percent Model on AOI and VLI, the Coppock indicator, Dow theory, the A/D line and others.

These methods are shown to work well on the AOI and the Gold Index, but the MACD is not as reliable on the All Industrials Index or the All Resources Index.

STRATEGY

A general strategy for trading investment companies and index-linked products is to buy when the market turns up and convert to cash when the market turns down. This way we avoid being trapped in any long-term downtrends, and hopefully re-enter the market at a lower price than when we quit. Alternatively, we may prefer to hold our investments in down turns, but protect them through buying index put warrants.

Index Warrants

Call and put index warrants are available on the AOI, while a single call warrant is available on the Gold Index (see Chapter 21).

For the AOI, we could adopt a policy of taking each up trade and down trade through the purchase of call and put index warrants respectively on a valid weekly MACD signal, and quit each trade using either the 250 point target profit stop, or the percentage profit trailing stop with a 250 point floor and 5% retracement. The index warrants offer an attractive gearing on the AOI of about three times.

For the Gold Index, we could adopt a policy of taking each up trade through the purchase of index call warrants on a valid weekly MACD signal, and quit each trade using the percentage profit trailing stop with a 175 point floor and 40% retracement.

Although there is currently no put warrant available on the Gold Index, put warrants are available on Normandy Mining, a major gold producer. Similarly, there are put and call options available on each of the gold producers Acacia, Newcrest and Normandy. Thus on a confirmed downtrend we have several possibilities:

- Stand aside and wait for the next uptrend.

- Buy Normandy put warrants.

- Short sell Normandy shares.

- Buy Acacia, Newcrest or Normandy put options.

- Write (sell) Acacia, Newcrest or Normandy call options.

The Gold Index has a high volatility, which results in a high delta for the index warrant, and consequently good profits on the index warrant in uptrends.

Investment Companies

Investment companies like AFIC, Argo and Milton out-perform the relevant accumulation indices as a result of good management, but also through compounding of returns. The impressive compound annual return figures of around 15% can only be achieved when all bonus and rights issues are taken up, and dividends are reinvested in the company. Thus if we have invested in, say, AFIC on a market upturn, it is probably intended as a long-term investment. Consequently, in market downtrends we could hedge against paper losses in the investment companies through trading AOI put warrants.

Investment companies trade at both a discount and premium to their net asset backing. Until the past two or three years prices were typically around a 10% discount, but in recent times they have climbed to premiums as high as 10%. It is useful to monitor the net asset backing figures which are published monthly, and possibly make purchases when the company is trading near its historic maximum discount with a view to either holding, or selling later at a premium.

Index-Linked Companies

BAT follows the AOI very closely, so we could adopt a policy of trading each uptrend in the AOI through the purchase of BAT shares, taking signals as for the AOI index warrants above. It is not possible to short BAT, so when the market turns down we convert to cash and put funds into an interest-bearing account with our broker to earn rates equivalent to the 90 Day Bank Bill rate. These funds are then available at 24-hour call and ready to reinvest on the next buy signal.

Alternatively, in downtrends we could maintain our holding in BAT, and hedge any loss through buying AOI put warrants. Profits made can be reinvested in BAT, as a form of compounding returns.

Index-Linked Funds

The index-linked funds allow us a choice of which index to replicate, i.e. the AOI, All Industrials Index, All Resources Index, etc. We need to monitor the appropriate index, and then invest cash in the funds on a confirmed uptrend.

When the trend ends we can switch into a cash fund, and be ready to enter the index-linked fund on the next uptrend. Index-linked funds offer a gearing to the underlying index of one times.

Alternatively, in downtrends we could maintain our holding in the index-linked funds, and hedge any loss through buying AOI put warrants.

RISK

There is a risk attached to each method of trading, with the index warrants having the highest return and highest risk. If the market turns against us then we quit on the next MACD signal, but this will involve a loss which is magnified by the warrant gearing as discussed in Chapter 27.

A lower-risk strategy is to buy BAT with the intent of holding it and reinvesting dividends, and so achieve returns equivalent to the All Ordinaries Accumulation Index. On confirmed downtrends we could trade AOI put warrants using the weekly MACD rules discussed above.

A similar low-risk strategy can be adopted with other index-linked funds.

Chapter 29

AN OVERALL PLAN FOR PORTFOLIO GROWTH

TO BUILD A portfolio and keep it growing, it is essential to give some thought to an overall plan, and to implement that plan over a number of years.

The investment plan chosen will depend upon many factors including age, income and job security, financial commitments, interest in the market, and time available to monitor the market.

At one end of the scale are the active traders or investors who manage their own portfolios, and devour market news to constantly monitor and change their holdings. At the other end are the passive investors who rely upon financial advisers to manage their portfolios, and whose contact with the market is the six-monthly, or annual, visit to the adviser to fine-tune the portfolio.

Between these two extremes are those people who enjoy following the market and do some trading, and choose some of their own investments, while also using a financial adviser to manage the remainder of their longer-term investments. The Over 50s and retirees tend to fall into this latter group. They need to spend some time keeping abreast of the market to help them to talk sensibly with their financial advisers.

Retirees are adverse to risk, so should carefully follow the rule, "do not put all your eggs in one basket". Thus a common strategy is for them to invest in several managed funds with different fund managers, covering both balanced and equity-type funds.

The critical reader will have noticed the progression through this book from analysis of the indices to discussion of index warrants, investment companies and managed funds which carry differing degrees of risk. Emphasis is upon doing our own analysis, making our own product selection, choosing the timing of entries and exits, and building confidence in our financial acumen and understanding of the markets.

A SUGGESTED GROWTH PORTFOLIO PLAN

Following the topics covered in this book, some suggestions are given to build a growing portfolio. The plan is applicable to people of any age group, and readers are encouraged to modify it to their own situation. (Selection of individual stocks for a portfolio is outside the scope of this book and needs to be discussed with a stockbroker or financial adviser.)

1. Make holdings in investment companies like AFIC, Argo, Milton and Templeton Global Growth Fund. Plan to take up all bonus and rights issues and participate in dividend reinvestment plans. These are long-term holdings and are not to be traded. Try to buy them when they are trading at a discount to net asset backing. Historically, the assets in these companies grow at around 15% compound per annum.

2. Make investments in index-linked funds like BAT or managed funds of your choosing. Decide whether to hold as long-term investments, or switch on confirmed downtrends to cash holdings, or protect them with AOI put warrants.

3. Consider subscribing to major new floats, or purchasing shares in a float's first week of trading (but seek advice from a stockbroker first). There are typically three or four of these floats each year, so gradually we can build up a quality portfolio including these stocks.

4. Seek out the best companies at any time for investment purposes. There are many excellent books to assist in this area, including those by Hewat and Connelly.

5. For those who enjoy trading, set aside some cash for this purpose. It is prudent to limit the amount committed to trading activities to, say, 20% of the total portfolio value. This trading may involve AOI call and put warrants in uptrends and downtrends. Decide what strategy to use in quitting trades, the types of stops to use, and consequently the broker to use in executing these stops.

6. Buy AOI put warrants on confirmed downtrends in the market to protect the value of other investments. Reinvest profits in stocks like the investment companies and BAT which should recover in the next uptrend.

7. Have a list of favourite stocks to buy on any slump. The October 1997 mini-crash was a classic example which most people missed, as it happened

so quickly. The investment companies and BAT should be on this list. If a quality stock falls, say, 15% to 20% for no reason other than general market gloom, a buying opportunity exists.

The book suggests a variety of ways to trade and invest in the local and overseas markets. The above plan is simple and has been profitable in the past. It is offered as food for thought for those willing and happy to manage their own portfolios.

WORKSHEETS

To follow the methods outlined in the book it is helpful to use worksheets which are filled in each week, or each month, with the relevant data.

Table 29.1 lists suggested data to be kept to provide an overview of the market. Weekly values are kept on the AOI, DJIA and VLI, and a number of indicators are applied to the AOI from which the new market trends can be determined. Monthly data is kept on the Rule of 20 and monthly Coppock indicator.

TABLE 29.1 Worksheet For All Ordinaries Index

Week ending	
AOI value	
Call warrant values	
Put warrant values	
DJIA value	
VLI value	
Indicators on AOI	
MACD	
3.5 Percent Model	
Coppock	
Advance/Decline line	
Dow theory trend	
Others	
3.5 Percent Model on VLI	
Monthly data	
Coppock	
Rule of 20	

Similar worksheets can be kept for the Gold Index, etc.

Chapter 30

LADY LUCK

ARE YOU A LUCKY person? Do you win the Melbourne Cup sweep at work, or the Chook Raffle at bowls?

There is an element of luck in stock market trading, though the professionals talk more in terms of taking only those trades where the odds are strongly in their favour.

As an example of luck in the trading context, consider again the weekly MACD on AOI using 250 point profit target stops as discussed in Chapter 16. Table 16.1 lists the profit results from each of the 23 legs, while Table 30.1 lists the relevant details of these first eight legs.

TABLE 30.1 Profit On Weekly All Ordinaries Index

No.	Leg Dir.	Date Opened	Profit (%)	$1,000 Growth			
1	Down	24/8/90	17.0	1,170			
2	Up	1/2/91	19.2	1,395	1,192		
3	Down	23/8/91	-6.5	1,304	1,114	935	
4	Up	25/10/91	-3.5	1,258	1,075	902	
5	Down	6/12/91	-5.1	1,194	1,020	856	
6	Up	1/5/92	-1.2	1,180	1,008	846	
7	Down	10/7/92	15.2	1,359	1,162	974	1,152
8	Up	11/12/92	16.7	1,586	1,356	1,137	1,344

The figures in the right-hand segment of Table 30.1 show the growth of a $1,000 investment at various starting points. Thus if we started trading at leg 1, then after leg 8 the $1,000 has grown to $1,586. Similarly, if we started at leg 2, then after leg 8 the $1,000 has grown to $1,356.

The unlucky person would start trading at leg 3 and after leg 6 the initial $1,000 has diminished to $846. That same person has followed the system correctly, but has been caught in a string of four consecutive losses, which can occur with a system that is right 50% of the time. What does that unfortunate person do at trade 7? The really unlucky person decides to give the system away, only to see the very profitable legs 7 and 8 slip by. The unlucky but disciplined person will continue trading, and feel very relieved to get on board trades 7 and 8, thereby recouping the losses.

The truly lucky person will start trading at leg 1 and take leg 2. Then a posting to Timbuktu will cause him to stop trading for the rest of 1991, and on returning in 1992 begin trading again at leg 7.

A lucky person will begin trading at leg 7, trade happily through to leg 23 and never regret using the system.

* * * * * * *

This little exercise demonstrates the usefulness of back-testing, and knowing all the subtle nuances of the system being used. There are always losses in a system. How we handle them is what counts, which is why the risk and money management factors discussed in Chapter 26 are so important.

Chapter 31

STOCK MARKET SOFTWARE AND DATA SUPPLIERS

TO PERFORM TECHNICAL analysis using a computer it is necessary to obtain historic data and process this with charting software. The data is then updated each day to keep the analysis current, and allows us to watch for MACD and other signals on a daily or weekly basis.

There are a number of Australian suppliers of software for technical analysis, as well as data suppliers. The November 1996 inaugural edition of *Shares* magazine, the *ASX Information Directory 1997* and the May/June 1998 edition of *Your Trading Edge*, all give comprehensive lists of suppliers and cover:

- Real-time data, i.e. price data during the trading session.

- Delayed information, i.e. close-of-day data.

- World Wide Web, i.e. free and pay-to-use information on financial markets in Australia and around the world.

- Charting software and trading systems, i.e. display downloaded data and perform technical analysis.

SOFTWARE

Popular charting and technical trading software along with suppliers and prices are:

> METASTOCK Phone: 1800 777 972 *or* (03) 5443 2435
> Cost: $595

SUPERCHARTS	Phone: 1800 777 972 *or* (02) 9879 7033
	Cost: $565
INSIGHT TRADER	Phone: (02) 4751 2932 *or* 1800 777 972
	Cost: $295
EZY CHARTS	Phone: 1800 777 972
	Cost: $199
STOCK EASY	Phone: (07) 3216 2240
	Cost: $199

The software suppliers often provide a free demonstration disk to allow a user to get a feel of the package before purchase.

The charting packages cover four main areas:

1. Displaying charts.

2. Technical indicators.

3. Signal alerts.

4. Portfolio management.

MetaStock and Supercharts cover the first three areas very well, and allow the user to build their own technical indicators and do back-testing. Neither have a portfolio management module.

Insight Trader, Ezy Charts and Stock Easy cover all four areas, but are limited to a set of pre-programmed technical indicators.

An important consideration is documentation and support. The software comes with documentation ranging from minimal to comprehensive, and most have built-in "Help" facilities. Software users find the Australian products to be better supported when a problem develops.

DATA PROVIDERS

Data providers supply a complete package of all ASX stocks, indices, warrants and futures, plus a selection of overseas indices and commodity prices. We refer to this below as "The Lot". A smaller selection can be chosen at lesser cost.

196

Each data provider can either deliver data in compatible formats for each of the five software packages, or provide conversion software for this purpose. They also provide historic data going back five years or more for a fee.

Some data providers deliver the data via a phone modem, others via the Internet or email. Again, some data providers use different cost rates, depending on whether the data is provided before or after midnight for each trading day.

If we do analysis on the weekend, and monitor prices at the close of each day, then the cheapest way of buying data is to take it after midnight via the Internet.

Some popular close-of-day data providers and indicative prices are listed below.

ALMAX   *Ph*: (03) 9561 7066

  Web site: www.almax.com.au
  The Lot: $75/month or $900 p.a.
  100 items: $240 p.a. (An item is one stock, or one index, etc.)
  Minimum subscription: $199 p.a.

DIAL & CHART   *Ph*: (03) 9569 8924

  Web site: www.dialchart.com.au
  The Lot (excluding overseas markets):
      Before midnight: $330 p.a.
      After midnight: $150 p.a.

EIS   *Ph*: 1800 777 972

  The Lot: $70/month or $840 p.a.
  100 items: $25/month or $300 p.a.
  Minimum subscription: $10 plus 15¢ per item per month.

PARITECH   *Ph*: (03) 9486 6511

  The Lot (but no overseas data available): $25/month or $300 p.a.

ODDS (OZSURF DATA DOWN-LOADING SYSTEM)   *Ph*: 1800 244 845

  Web site: www.odds.com.au
  The Lot: $600 p.a.
  The first year's subscription to ODDS includes 11 years of historic data.

TAKE TIME TO DECIDE

For readers intending to purchase software and data to allow them to perform technical analysis, some guidance is usually required. From time to time *Personal Investment* and *Shares* magazines run articles on this topic.

The ATAA has conducted surveys of data suppliers and also of software suppliers which are available from the Honorary Secretary on (02) 9337 5673. In the *ATAA Software Survey* the following advice was given:

> "Experience has shown that the best course in selecting software is to decide which markets are to be traded and then determine which data sources are available for those markets. The formats in which the data is available should then be determined and software selected that can handle the available formats. Finally, the computer and modem hardware should be chosen to accommodate the software and the data sources used."

Requirements

To determine the uptrends and downtrends in the AOI and Gold Index as discussed in this book, a set of requirements ranging from minimum to more complex is:

1. Manual System

   - Weekly data on DJIA, VLI, spot gold price, AOI and Gold Index.

   - 3.5 Percent Model on VLI and AOI.

   - Hand-drawn charts.

   - Rule of 20.

2. Computer System

   - Daily data on DJIA, VLI, spot gold price, AOI and Gold Index. Weekly VLI may have to be manually collected from the media or a broker, if not available from a data supplier.

   - MACD, 3.5 Percent Model.

   - 3.5 Percent Model needs to be calculated by hand to check the validity of an approximated computer system.

- Ezy Chart, Stock Easy or Insight Trader software is a suitable starting point, and each has several indicators including MACD. Ezy Charts calculates the A/D line and charts it, while Insight Trader has the Coppock indicator and charts A/D as a pre-programmed indicator.

3. Advanced Computer System

- Daily and weekly data as above.

- Indicators as above, plus software capable of calculating Coppock indicator, back-testing capability, and software or data supplier like Almax to provide A/D line chart.

- Capability of building and back-testing custom indicators.

- MetaStock or SuperCharts 4 required.

ATAA

The Australian Technical Analysts Association is a national forum for learning and exchanging ideas. It holds monthly meetings in Adelaide, Brisbane, Canberra, Melbourne, Perth, Sydney and Toowoomba, and publishes a bi-monthly Journal.

The ATAA address is: GPO Box 2774, Sydney 1043, and contact phone numbers are: (02) 9436 1610 and (02) 9337 5673. An information pack, including a free copy of the Journal, is available on request.

HARDWARE

The hardware required to run the charting software is an IBM compatible 486 or better computer with Windows 95.

Also required is a modem for receiving information from a data provider, and a printer for drawing charts, etc.

Chapter 32

CONCLUSIONS

THE THRUST OF THIS book is to assist readers gain confidence in making their own investment decisions, with the goal of building and protecting their portfolios. The general philosophy can be summed up as: "buy the uptrends and sell the downs".

We take the big picture by trading and investing in financial products which enable us to trade the indices, rather than individual stocks. This allows us to match or better these benchmarks, and minimises the amount of time required to monitor and analyse the markets to reach our investment decisions.

For trading, it is shown that worthwhile profits can be made using a system which is right 50% of the time, provided discipline and predetermined rules are used in trading. Profitability comes through quitting the losses early, but riding the winners as long as possible. Stops are used which are matched to the index behaviour and the analysis system being used.

The book has worked through a number of steps in implementing an overall investment plan:

1. Decide which technical indicators to use. Check their profitability on weekly AOI data, and decide what stops to use to maximise profits. Back-test the indicators, and check any optimising parameters from time to time.

2. Understand the pros and cons of the available put and call warrants on the AOI, and the call warrant on the Gold Index.

3. Be familiar with index-linked products and investment companies available on the ASX such as BAT, AFIC, Argo, Milton, TGG, etc. Also be familiar with index-linked managed funds.

4. Determine the level of risk/reward you are prepared to accept, which in turn determines the type of trading strategy to use.

If a high risk/reward system is chosen, then AOI call warrants could be bought during uptrends, and AOI put warrants could be bought during downtrends.

A low risk/reward strategy could be to buy stocks like AFIC, Argo, Milton, TGG, etc. when the market is depressed and the stocks are selling at a discount to net asset backing. Then simply hold the stocks, always take up new issues, and participate in any dividend reinvestment schemes.

Between these extremes there are many shades of grey. For example, one medium risk/reward system could be to buy the BAT on uptrends, and hold during downtrends but also buy AOI put warrants to profit from the fall in the market. When the market turns up again, the profits from the put warrants could be used to buy more BAT, thereby compounding the holding.

5. Decide on the money management procedures to be adopted. The risk and money management rules must be clearly defined, written down, memorised, and adhered to.

6. Choose the charting software, data provider and hardware to implement the trading methods.

The whole exercise of monitoring, analysing, trading and investing needs to be enjoyable, otherwise it is best to hand the process over to an investment adviser to purchase some of the quality stocks, and managed funds, on offer.

Chapter 33

RESOURCES

BOOKS AND ARTICLES

Armstrong, M.   *How To Chart Your Way To Success On The Stock Market*, Rydge Publications Pty Ltd, Sydney, NSW, 1984.

Bolton-Smith, D.   "Some Of The Best Indicators For The 1994/5 Bear Market", *ATAA Journal*, March 1995.

Connelly, D.   *The Over 50s Investor*, Wrightbooks, Elsternwick, Victoria, 1997.

Dunstan, B.   *The Art Of Investment*, Financial Review Library, Melbourne, Victoria, 1992.

Guppy, D.   *Share Trading: An Approach To Buying And Selling*, Wrightbooks, Elsternwick, Victoria, 1996.

Hewat, T.   *The Intelligent Investor's Guide to Share Buying*, 4th Edition, Wrightbooks, Elsternwick, Victoria, 1996.

Jiler, William L.   *How Charts Can Help You In The Stock Market*, Trendline, USA, 1968.

Krastins, I.   *Listen To The Market*, McGraw Book Company, Sydney, NSW, 1990.

LeBeau, C., Lucas, D.W.   *Computer Analysis Of The Futures Market*, Business One Irwin, Homewood, Illinois, 1992.

Lee, C.F.,   *Security Analysis And Portfolio Management*,
Finnerty, J.E.,   Scott, Foresman Company, Glenview, Illinois, 1990.
Worth, D.H.

Leuthold, S.   "Coppock and VLT Momentum: A Low Risk Buy Signal",
                    The IFTA Journal, 1994 Edition.

Meani, R.   *The Australian Investor's Guide To Charting*,
                    Wrightbooks, Elsternwick, Victoria, 1996.

Nicholson, C.   "The Poor Man's Coppock Indicator",
                    ATAA Journal, March and May 1995.

Pascoe, M.   "A Fundamental Fiasco",
                    Your Trading Edge, Jan/Feb 1998.

Pring, M.J.   *Technical Analysis Explained*,
                    McGraw-Hill Inc., New York, N.Y., 1991.

Sands, R.   "A Taste Of Turtle Trading",
                    ATAA Journal, July 1997.

Schwager, J.D.   *Market Wizards*,
                    HarperBusiness, New York, N.Y., 1993.

Tate, C.   *Understanding Futures Trading in Australia*,
                    Wrightbooks, Elsternwick, Victoria, 1998.

Temby, A.C.   *Trading Stock Options And Warrants*,
                    Wrightbooks, Elsternwick, Victoria, 1997.

Tharp, V.K.   "Your Performance Trading Edge",
                    ATAA Journal, January 1994.

                    "Judgement Biases – How They Affect Your Performance".
                    ATAA Journal, March 1995.

Wheelan, A.H.   *Study Helps in Point and Figure Technique*,
                    Fraser Publishing Company, Vermont, 1989.

Wilder, J.W.Jr.   *New Concepts In Technical Trading Systems*,
                    Hunter Publishing Company, Winston-Salem, North
                    Carolina, 1974.

Zweig, M.E.   *Winning On Wall Street*,
                   Warner Books, New York, N.Y., 1986.

MAGAZINES AND NEWSPAPERS

Several monthly magazines are available from newsagents which give a commentary on various aspects of the stock market. Two such magazines are *Personal Investment* and *Shares*.

Readers who are interested in technical analysis and trading will find the following two helpful:

> *Your Trading Edge* – the magazine for traders in futures, options, forex, stocks and commodities – available from the Sydney Futures Exchange, Level 3, 30-32 Grosvenor St, Sydney, NSW, telephone (02) 9256 0555 or 1800 641 588.

> *Australian Technical Analysts Association Journal*, GPO Box 2774, Sydney, NSW, 1043.

The "Smart Money" section in the weekend *Australian Financial Review* contains topical, and informative, articles on a range of subjects.

Appendix A

FORMULA FOR
TECHNICAL ANALYSIS

THE MATHEMATICS OF the technical indicators used needs be defined both for completeness, and because different texts may express it in different ways, and different software packages may calculate the indicators in different ways.

SuperCharts 4 has been used in this book for all the analysis and optimising studies. SuperCharts 4 has a suite of custom indicators covering SMA, MACD, DMI, ADX, etc. It also allows the user to program their own indicators and trading logic with QuickEditor Easy Language.

This Appendix gives the mathematics of the indicators, and also the code to write the indicators in QuickEditor Easy Language. Readers using SuperCharts can thus verify the book analysis, or extend the analysis in ways of interest to them.

Readers with other software packages will find the QuickEditor Easy Language gives a guide as to how to program the indicators in their own software.

Table A.1 lists some of the relevant QuickEditor Easy Language code and its meaning, which is used in defining the indicators.

TABLE A.1   QuickEditor Easy Language

QuickEditor Easy Language Code	Meaning
[N]	Value N periods ago
Close	Closing price
C	Abbreviation for "Close"

QuickEditor Easy Language Code	Meaning
Crosses	Used with reserved words Above, Below, Under and Over
High	High value of a price bar
H	Abbreviation for "High"
Highest(price,N)	Highest price value over past N data
Low	Low value of a price bar
L	Abbreviation for "Low"
Lowest(price,N)	Lowest price value over past N data

SINGLE MOVING AVERAGE

One of the simplest, yet most useful, technical indicators is the single moving average (SMA).

For close price data the SMA is:

$$SMA = \frac{\left(sum\ of\ N\ close\ prices \right)}{N}$$

where:

N = number of data being used in the SMA

QuickEditor Easy Language:

SMA = Average(close,N)

System Equity with parameters len1, len2

For 20-week SMA set len1 = 1, len2 = 20

Long entry if: Average(c,len1) crosses above Average(c,len2)

Short entry if: Average(c,len1) crosses below Average(c,len2)

Filter requires len2 SMA to have reached peak or trough:

Long entry if: (Average(c,len1) > Average(c,len2)) *AND*

(Average(c,len2) > Average(c,len2)[1])

Long exit if: Average(c,len1) crosses below Average(c,len2)

Short entry if: (Average(c,len1) < Average(c,len2)) *AND*

               (Average(c,len2) < Average(c,len2)[1])

Short exit if: Average(c,len1) crosses above Average(c,len2)

DOUBLE MOVING AVERAGE

QuickEditor Easy Language:

Long entry if: Average(c,len1) crosses above Average(c,len2)

Short entry if: Average(c,len1) crosses below Average(c,len2)

BASIC TRIPLE MOVING AVERAGE

Open trades when the 9-day SMA crosses the 18-day SMA, and close trades when the 4-day SMA crosses the 9-day SMA.

QuickEditor Easy Language:

Long entry if: Average(c,9) crosses above Average(c,18)

Long exit if: Average(c,4) crosses below Average(c,9)

Short entry if: Average(c,9) crosses below Average(c,18)

Short exit if: Average(c,4) crosses above Average(c,9)

ADVANCED TRIPLE MOVING AVERAGE

QuickEditor Easy Language:

Long entry if: (Average(c,4) > Average(c,9)) *AND*

               (Average(c,9) > Average(c,18))

Long exit if: Average(c,4) crosses below Average(c,9)

Short entry if: (Average(c,4) < Average(c,9)) *AND*

               (Average(c,9) < Average(c,18))

Short exit if: Average(c,4) crosses above Average(c,9)

EXPONENTIAL SMOOTHING

Exponential smoothing is an alternative mathematical procedure which discounts the older data. Exponential smoothing is an iterative procedure whereby each new smoothed value is calculated by adding a portion of the new data to the preceding smoothed value. The smoothing effectively gives current data a higher weighting than older data, with the weighting on old data decaying to zero.

For the data stream P_1, P_2, .. P_N with P_1 being the most recent, the smoothed values are S_1, S_2 .. S_N .., where:

$$S_1 = S_2 + \ltimes (P_1 - S_2)$$

Smoothing factor is $\ltimes = \dfrac{2}{1 + N}$

where:

N = the number of data in the calculation

QuickEditor Easy Language:

EMA = Xaverage(close,N)

WEIGHTED MOVING AVERAGE

The common method of weighting a moving average is to weight data according to its age. Applying a N day weighted average to the data stream P_1, P_2, .. P_N with P_1 being the most recent, then:

$$\text{Weighted average} = \frac{[NP_1 + (N-1)P_2 + ..P_N]}{N}$$

QuickEditor Easy Language:

Weighted average = Waverage(close,N)

MOVING AVERAGE CONVERGENCE DIVERGENCE (MACD)

The 12-data and 26-data exponential smoothing values are calculated as EMA_{12} and EMA_{26}, and the difference obtained as $EMA_{12} - EMA_{26}$. This difference is the MACD line and moves above and below zero. The MACD line is exponentially smoothed using 9-data smoothing, and this is called the signal line. The MACD line crosses up and down through the signal line, and these crossovers are taken as the start and finish of the stock trends. The complete notation for the MACD indicator is MACD(12,26,9).

Thus when the MACD line crosses above the signal line the trend is up, while when the MACD line crosses below the signal line the trend is down.

MACD(12,26,9) becomes:

MACD line $= \text{EMA}_{12} - \text{EMA}_{26}$

Signal line $=$ 9-data EMA on MACD line

QuickEditor Easy Language:

The MACD is programmed as a custom indicator MACD(price,fast,slow).

Open long if: MACD(c,12,26) crosses above Xaverage(MACD(c,12,26),9)

Open short if: MACD(c,12,26) crosses below Xaverage(MACD(c,12,26),9)

DIRECTIONAL MOVEMENT INDICATOR (DMI) AND AVERAGE DIRECTIONAL MOVEMENT INDEX (ADX)

To calculate the DMI it is first necessary to understand the concepts of "directional movement" and "true range". When the trend is up, today's high should be above yesterday's high, and their difference is the "up" directional movement, defined as $+DM$. Similarly, when the trend is down, today's low should be below yesterday's low, and their difference is the "down" directional movement, defined as $-DM$.

Directional movement is the largest part of today's range that is outside yesterday's range. The various possibilities are shown in Figure A1 overleaf.

The true range (TR) is the largest of:

Today's high – today's low

Today's high – yesterday's close

Yesterday's close – today's low

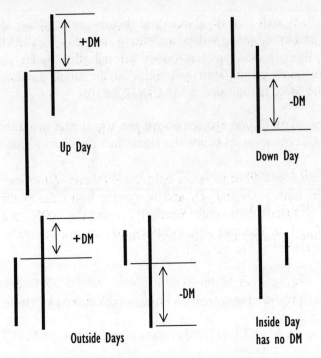

Gap day is the same as an up or down day

FIGURE A.1 Definition of Directional Movement

Each day has a directional index DI defined as $\frac{DM}{TR}$. These values are normally calculated over 14 days and then separated into up DM days and down DM days. The resulting 14 day up DI is $+DI_{14}$ and the down DI is $-DI_{14}$ where:

$$+DI_{14} = \frac{+DM_{14}}{TR_{14}}$$

$$-DI_{14} = \frac{-DM_{14}}{TR_{14}}$$

By convention the $-DM_{14}$ values are positive. Thus when the $+DI_{14}$ and $-DI_{14}$ are plotted together they form crossovers. When the $+DI_{14}$ crosses above the $-DI_{14}$ an uptrend is signalled, while when the $-DI_{14}$ crosses above the $+DI_{14}$ a downtrend is signalled. The $+DI_{14}$ and $-DI_{14}$ terms comprise the DMI.

The ADX is calculated as:

$$ADX_{14} = \frac{|(+DI_{14}) - (-DI_{14})|}{(+DI_{14}) + (-DI_{14})}$$

The ADX_{14} is a measure of the strength of the trend. When the stock is moving sideways there will be little difference between $+DI_{14}$ and $-DI_{14}$. However, as the stock develops either an uptrend or downtrend, the difference between $+DI_{14}$ and $-DI_{14}$ will widen and ADX_{14} will increase in value. When the trend starts to turn over the $+DI_{14}$ and $-DI_{14}$ will begin to converge again, and the ADX_{14} will fall.

Each of $+DI_{14}$, $-DI_{14}$ and ADX_{14} is multiplied by 100, so they are all plotted within the scale 0 to 100.

The ADX is used as a filter to select only the $+DI$ and $-DI$ crossovers where the ADX is below both $+DI$ and $-DI$ and is moving upwards, as this indicates the beginning of a sustainable trend. Similarly, when the ADX is above both the $+DI$ and $-DI$ and turns down, this indicates that the present trend is weakening, and is an opportune time to quit a trade.

The primary interpretation of the ADX is that a rising ADX infers a trend (either up or down) is strengthening, while a falling ADX infers a trend is weakening or becoming a sideways move.

QuickEditor Easy Language:

    Custom indicators are available as
        DMIPlus(N), DMIMinus(N), DMI(N) and ADX(N)

MACD WITH DMI/ADX FILTER

Parameter "len" is given a numeric value, typically 14 for daily data and 10 for weekly data.

QuickEditor Easy Language:

Long entry if: (MACD(c,12,26) > Xaverage(MACD(c,12,26),9)) *AND*
             (DMIPlus(len) > DMIMinus(len)) *AND*
             (ADX(len) > ADX(len)[1])

Long exit if: MACD(c,12,26) crosses below Xaverage(MACD(c,12,26),9)

Short entry if: (MACD(c,12,26) < Xaverage(MACD(c,12,26),9)) *AND*
             (DMIPlus(len) < DMIMinus(len)) *AND*
             (ADX(len) > ADX(len)[1])

Short exit if: MACD(c,12,26) crosses above Xaverage(MACD(c,12,26),9)

TURTLES TRADING

A new uptrend is defined on a new 20-day high, and the trend continues until there is a 10-day low.

A new downtrend is defined on a new 20-day low, and the trend continues until there is a 10-day high.

QuickEditor Easy Language:

Long entry if: High > highest(high,19)[1]

Long exit if: Low < lowest(low,9)[1]

Short entry if: Low < lowest(low,19)[1])

Short exit if: High > highest(high,9)[1]

PERCENT MODEL

A new uptrend is defined when the close price moves up more than Y% from the previous trough. Similarly, a new downtrend is defined when the close price moves down more than Y% from the previous peak.

QuickEditor Easy Language:

For a 3.5 Percent Model, set Y = 3.5

Long entry if: (Close > (1+Y/100)*lowest(c,3)[1]) *AND* (c > c[1])

Short entry if: (Close < (1-Y/100)*highest(c,3)[1]) *AND* (c < c[1])

Note that this logic detects a move from a peak or trough that occurred within the past three periods, but it may not pick the correct peak or trough if they occur more than three periods earlier.

MOMENTUM OR RATE OF CHANGE (ROC)

Momentum M is defined as:

$$M = P_t - P_{t-N}$$

where:

P_t is today's close price and P_{t-N} is the close price N data ago

Momentum moves up and down through the zero line as prices move from uptrends to downtrends. Momentum gives an up signal when it crosses above the zero line, and a down signal when it crosses below the zero line.

QuickEditor Easy Language:

Momentum = close – close[N]

COPPOCK INDICATOR

The Coppock indicator is the 10-month weighted average of:

11-month ROC + 14-month ROC

The ROC values are expressed as percentages.

QuickEditor Easy Language:

Coppock = Waverage(100*((c-c[11])/c[11]+ (c-c[14])/c[14]),10)

Open long if: (Waverage(100*((c-c[11])/c[11]+
                (c-c[14])/c[14]),10) < 0) *AND*
                (Waverage(100*((c-c[11])/c[11]+
                (c-c[14])/c[14]),10) >
                Waverage(100*((c-c[11])/c[11]+
                (c-c[14])/c[14]),10)[1])

Open short if: (Waverage(100*((c-c[11])/c[11]+
                (c-c[14])/c[14]),10) > 0) *AND*
                (Waverage(100*((c-c[11])/c[11]+
                (c-c[14])/c[14]),10) <
                Waverage(100*((c-c[11])/c[11]+
                (c-c[14])/c[14]),10)[1])

When using N-period SMA to define peaks and troughs:

Open long if: Waverage(100*((c-c[11])/c[11]+
(c-c[14])/c[14]),10) crosses above
average(Waverage(100*((c-c[11])/c[11]+
(c-c[14])/c[14]),10),N)

Open short if: Waverage(100*((c-c[11])/c[11]+
(c-c[14])/c[14]),10) crosses below
average(Waverage(100*((c-c[11])/c[11]+
(c-c[14])/c[14]),10),N)

POOR MAN'S COPPOCK INDICATOR

The Poor Man's Coppock Indicator is defined as:

10-data SMA – 20-data SMA

QuickEditor Easy Language:

Poor Man's Coppock = average(c,10) – average(c,20)

Appendix B

WEEKLY VALUE LINE INDEX OVER 5.5 YEARS

TABLE B.1 LISTS the weekly closing prices of the VLI over the 5.5 years from 11/9/92 to 27/3/98 (reading the date and price down each column, then across to the next column on the page), and can be used as input to the various indicators to determine trends. The signals for the start of the uptrends and downtrends, as defined by the 3.5 Percent Model on the VLI, are marked in the table as Up or Do.

TABLE B.1   Weekly VLI Values

Date	Price	Date	Price	Date	Price
11/9/92	249.2	11/12/92	261.4	12/3/93	279.2
18/9/92	250.0	18/12/92	263.6	19/3/93	278.7
25/9/92	245.5	25/12/92	262.9	26/3/93	277.9
2/10/92	245.2	1/1/93	266.7	2/4/93	274.8
9/10/92	240.6	8/1/93	264.5	9/4/93	272.8
16/10/92	242.2	15/1/93	270.0	16/4/93	275.8
23/10/92	246.4	22/1/93	272.5	23/4/93	271.7
30/10/92	249.3 Up	29/1/93	273.1	30/4/93	272.2
6/11/92	251.2	5/2/93	279.0	7/5/93	275.6
13/11/92	254.7	12/2/93	277.0	14/5/93	275.2
20/11/92	255.7	19/2/93	270.6	21/5/93	278.1
27/11/92	258.7	26/2/93	273.4	28/5/93	280.4
4/12/92	261.9	5/3/93	276.7	4/6/93	280.3

Date	Price	Date	Price	Date	Price
11/6/93	276.4	7/1/94	297.4	5/8/94	281.8
18/6/93	274.8	14/1/94	299.4	12/8/94	284.7 Up
25/6/93	275.4	21/1/94	300.8	19/8/94	286.8
2/7/93	278.1	28/1/94	302.6	26/8/94	292.0
9/7/93	278.2	4/2/94	298.8	2/9/94	292.5
16/7/93	278.6	11/2/94	299.6	9/9/94	291.5
23/7/93	276.6	18/2/94	299.4	16/9/94	293.9
30/7/93	278.4	25/2/94	298.0	23/9/94	286.4
6/8/93	280.0	4/3/94	298.7	30/9/94	287.9
13/8/93	280.7	11/3/94	299.8	7/10/94	282.9 Do
20/8/93	284.7	18/3/94	305.2	14/10/94	288.3
27/8/93	285.8	25/3/94	299.2	21/10/94	285.9
3/9/93	288.0	1/4/94	284.8 Do	28/10/94	288.3
10/9/93	286.0	8/4/94	286.9	4/11/94	284.1
17/9/93	284.5	15/4/94	283.6	11/11/94	281.1
24/9/93	285.4	22/4/94	281.0	18/11/94	279.1
1/10/93	287.8	29/4/94	286.0	25/11/94	271.4
8/10/93	288.6	6/5/94	283.8	2/12/94	273.1
15/10/93	293.3	13/5/94	278.3	9/12/94	266.6
22/10/93	290.6	20/5/94	282.5	16/12/94	272.5
29/10/93	293.2	27/5/94	283.7	23/12/94	275.3
5/11/93	286.9	3/6/94	285.9	30/12/94	277.5 Up
12/11/93	292.1	10/6/94	285.2	6/1/95	278.0
19/11/93	287.8	17/6/94	284.7	13/1/95	279.7
26/11/93	287.3	24/6/94	273.7	20/1/95	279.2
3/12/93	289.9	1/7/94	276.0	27/1/95	279.3
10/12/93	290.0	8/7/94	276.9	3/2/95	282.5
17/12/93	291.0	15/7/94	281.2	10/2/95	286.4
24/12/93	290.7	22/7/94	280.0	17/2/95	285.9
31/12/93	294.5	29/7/94	281.5	24/2/95	287.6

Date	Price	Date	Price	Date	Price
3/3/95	286.7	6/10/95	325.8	10/5/96	356.3
10/3/95	286.4	13/10/95	326.4	17/5/96	363.6
17/3/95	287.3	20/10/95	324.3	24/5/96	364.7
24/3/95	289.1	27/10/95	316.0 Do	31/5/96	361.8
31/3/95	292.0	3/11/95	323.8	7/6/96	360.0
7/4/95	293.7	10/11/95	324.9	14/6/96	357.3
14/4/95	296.1	17/11/95	325.5	21/6/96	353.1
21/4/95	295.0	24/11/95	325.6	28/6/96	354.3
28/4/95	297.8	1/12/95	329.3 Up	5/7/96	349.3 Do
5/5/95	298.4	8/12/95	330.8	12/7/96	339.7
12/5/95	302.4	15/12/95	328.0	19/7/96	335.2
19/5/95	301.0	22/12/95	328.9	26/7/96	330.8
26/5/95	301.9	29/12/95	331.0	2/8/96	340.6
2/6/95	304.5	5/1/96	330.9	9/8/96	342.6 Up
9/6/95	304.3	12/1/96	323.6	16/8/96	345.9
16/6/95	308.8	19/1/96	324.8	23/8/96	347.6
23/6/95	311.7	26/1/96	328.6	30/8/96	345.1
30/6/95	311.1	2/2/96	336.0	6/9/96	346.1
7/7/95	318.2	9/2/96	341.1	13/9/96	352.7
14/7/95	321.3	16/2/96	341.6	20/9/96	355.2
21/7/95	316.4	23/2/96	343.6	27/9/96	355.7
28/7/95	322.7	1/3/96	339.6	4/10/96	360.4
4/8/95	322.0	8/3/96	335.5	11/10/96	359.5
11/8/95	321.1	15/3/96	341.2	18/10/96	361.3
18/8/95	325.4	22/3/96	344.5	25/10/96	358.1
25/8/95	325.4	29/3/96	345.0	1/11/96	357.0
1/9/95	326.7	5/4/96	348.8	8/11/96	364.7
8/9/95	332.6	12/4/96	343.4	15/11/96	368.9
15/9/95	333.7	19/4/96	349.1	22/11/96	373.2
22/9/95	331.3	26/4/96	355.4	29/11/96	375.3
29/9/95	331.0	3/5/96	353.2	6/12/96	372.9

Date	Price	Date	Price	Date	Price
13/12/96	369.0	23/5/97	401.1	31/10/97	446.4 Do
20/12/96	374.5	30/5/97	405.0	7/11/97	448.7
27/12/96	375.9	6/6/97	410.7	14/11/97	444.8
3/1/97	376.2	13/6/97	419.5	21/11/97	453.9
10/1/97	380.8	20/6/97	420.7	28/11/97	450.1
17/1/97	385.9	27/6/97	419.1	5/12/97	458.2
24/1/97	382.9	4/7/97	428.3	12/12/97	443.4
31/1/97	385.5	11/7/97	432.1	19/12/97	443.7
7/2/97	385.3	18/7/97	434.3	26/12/97	439.9
14/2/97	391.4	25/7/97	438.2	2/1/98	455.0
21/2/97	389.7	1/8/97	444.5	9/1/98	431.7
28/2/97	385.3	8/8/97	443.0	26/1/98	443.5
7/3/97	391.7	15/8/97	436.9	23/1/98	441.3
14/3/97	388.8	22/8/97	441.9	30/1/98	447.3 Up
21/3/97	381.1	29/8/97	443.0	6/2/98	462.4
28/3/97	377.4 Do	5/9/97	453.1	13/2/98	469.1
4/4/97	369.8	12/9/97	456.5	20/2/98	473.0
11/4/97	365.2	19/8/97	464.5	27/2/98	480.0
18/4/97	371.0	26/9/97	464.4	6/3/98	482.9
25/4/97	365.4	3/10/97	473.6	13/3/98	489.4
2/5/97	385.6 Up	10/10/97	474.6	20/3/98	495.8
9/5/97	390.1	17/10/97	464.0	27/3/98	497.4
16/5/97	393.7	24/10/97	461.9		

Appendix C

WEEKLY ALL ORDINARIES INDEX OVER 7.5 YEARS

TABLE C.1 LISTS THE weekly closing prices of the AOI over the 7.5 years from 1/6/90 to 27/3/98, and can be used as input to the various indicators to determine trends. The signals for the start of the up and down trends, as defined by the 3.5 Percent Model on the AOI, are marked in the table as Up or Do.

TABLE C.1 Weekly AOI Values

Date	Price	Date	Price	Date	Price
1/6/90	1,514	31/8/90	1,508	30/11/90	1,320
8/6/90	1,504	7/9/90	1,479	7/12/90	1,336
15/6/90	1,503	14/9/90	1,480	14/12/90	1,310 Do
22/6/90	1,513	21/9/90	1,428	21/12/90	1,272
29/6/90	1,501	28/9/90	1,398	28/12/90	1,280
6/7/90	1,554	5/10/90	1,357	4/1/91	1,242
13/7/90	1,601	12/10/90	1,326	11/1/91	1,244
20/7/90	1,602	19/10/90	1,369	18/1/91	1,267
27/7/90	1,578	26/10/90	1,355	25/1/91	1,296 Up
3/8/90	1,590	2/11/90	1,291	1/2/91	1,303
10/8/90	1,569	9/11/90	1,329	8/2/91	1,340
17/8/90	1,543 Do	16/11/90	1340 Up	15/2/91	1,377
24/8/90	1,470	23/11/90	1,367	22/2/91	1,387

Date	Price	Date	Price	Date	Price
1/3/91	1,395	27/9/91	1,559	24/4/92	1,610
8/3/91	1,415	4/10/91	1,587	1/5/92	1,665 Up
15/3/91	1,446	11/10/91	1,555	8/5/92	1,664
22/3/91	1,428	18/10/91	1,618	15/5/92	1,661
29/3/91	1,444	25/10/91	1,642	22/5/92	1,685
5/4/91	1,456	1/11/91	1,684	29/5/92	1,678
12/4/91	1,456	8/11/91	1,696	5/6/92	1,675
19/4/91	1,520	15/11/91	1,677	12/6/92	1,651
26/4/91	1,538	22/11/91	1,643	19/6/92	1,634
3/5/91	1,518	29/11/91	1,606 Do	26/6/92	1,642
10/5/91	1,548	6/12/91	1,584	3/7/92	1,663
17/5/91	1,532	13/12/91	1,598	10/7/92	1,644
24/5/91	1,537	20/12/91	1,574	17/7/92	1,630
31/5/91	1,510	27/12/91	1,595	24/7/92	1,610 Do
7/6/91	1,478 Do	3/1/92	1,660 Up	31/7/92	1,616
14/6/91	1,507	10/1/92	1,668	7/8/92	1,587
21/6/91	1,512	17/1/92	1,674	14/8/92	1,549
28/6/91	1,506	24/1/92	1,616	21/8/92	1,559
5/7/91	1,536 Up	31/1/92	1,620	28/8/92	1,554
12/7/91	1,532	7/2/92	1,591 Do	4/9/92	1,530
19/7/91	1,551	14/2/92	1,619	11/9/92	1,501
26/7/91	1,563	21/2/92	1,622	18/9/92	1,524
2/8/91	1,583	28/2/92	1,614	25/9/92	1,496
9/8/91	1,584	6/3/92	1,605	2/10/92	1,483
16/8/91	1,567	13/3/92	1,588	9/10/92	1,466
23/8/91	1,541	20/3/92	1,584	16/10/92	1,420
30/8/91	1,540	27/3/92	1,576	23/10/92	1,456
6/9/91	1,572	3/4/92	1,566	30/10/92	1,426
13/9/91	1,568	10/4/92	1,582	6/11/92	1,423
20/9/91	1,563	17/4/92	1,590	13/11/92	1,372

Date	Price	Date	Price	Date	Price
20/11/92	1,410	25/6/93	1,700	28/1/94	2,260
27/11/92	1,451 Up	2/7/93	1,769	4/2/94	2,333
4/12/92	1,435	9/7/93	1,783	11/2/94	2,241 Do
11/12/92	1,501	16/7/93	1,800	18/2/94	2,223
18/12/92	1,516	23/7/93	1,807	25/2/94	2,149
25/12/92	1,536	30/7/93	1,844	4/3/94	2,117
1/1/93	1,550	6/8/93	1,842	11/3/94	2,153
8/1/93	1,502	13/8/93	1,856	18/3/94	2,164
15/1/93	1,525	20/8/93	1,927	25/3/94	2,152
22/1/93	1,523	27/8/93	1,945	1/4/94	2,053
29/1/93	1,528	3/9/93	1,952	8/4/94	2,082
5/2/93	1,543	10/9/93	1,942	15/4/94	2,081
12/2/93	1,604	17/9/93	1,926	22/4/94	2,043
19/2/93	1,595	24/9/93	1,947	29/4/94	2,066
26/2/93	1,610	1/10/93	1,973	6/5/94	2,004
5/3/93	1,614	8/10/93	2,026	13/5/94	2,070
12/3/93	1,662	15/10/93	2,074	20/5/94	2,104 Up
19/3/93	1,677	22/10/93	2,061	27/5/94	2,102
26/3/93	1,676	29/10/93	2,112	3/6/94	2,079
2/4/93	1,683	5/11/93	2,080	10/6/94	2,069
9/4/93	1,666	12/11/93	2,074	17/6/94	2,051
16/4/93	1,703	19/11/93	2,083	24/6/94	2,018 Do
23/4/93	1,703	26/11/93	2,043	1/7/94	1,966
30/4/93	1,682	3/12/93	2,047	8/7/94	1,965
7/5/93	1,685	10/12/93	2,085	15/7/94	2,058 Up
14/5/93	1,699	17/12/93	2,080	22/7/94	2,053
21/5/93	1,696	24/12/93	2,089	29/7/94	2,062
28/5/93	1,760	31/12/93	2,174	5/8/94	2,092
4/6/93	1,741	7/1/94	2,186	12/8/94	2,052
11/6/93	1,714	14/1/94	2,206	19/8/94	2,061
18/6/93	1,730	21/1/94	2,250	26/8/94	2,077

Date	Price	Date	Price	Date	Price
2/9/94	2,107	7/4/95	1,983	10/11/95	2,126
9/9/94	2,071	14/4/95	2,021	17/11/95	2,120
16/9/94	2,059	21/4/95	2,001	24/11/95	2,151 Up
23/9/94	2,028 Do	28/4/95	2,050	1/12/95	2,163
30/9/94	2,029	5/5/95	2,066	8/12/95	2,186
7/10/94	1,968	12/5/95	2,039	15/12/95	2,221
14/10/94	2,006	19/5/95	1,997	22/12/95	2,207
21/10/94	2,035	26/5/95	2,024	29/12/95	2,203
28/10/94	2,021	2/6/95	2,007	5/1/96	2,261
4/11/94	2,000	9/6/95	1,985 Do	12/1/96	2,239
11/11/94	1,952	16/6/95	1,974	19/1/96	2,247
18/11/94	1,922	23/6/95	2,026	26/1/96	2,254
25/11/94	1,910	30/6/95	2,017	2/2/96	2,293
2/12/94	1,880	7/7/95	2046 Up	9/2/96	2,272
9/12/94	1,851	14/7/95	2,114	16/2/96	2,297
16/12/94	1,897	21/7/95	2,122	23/2/96	2,264
23/12/94	1,909	28/7/95	2,120	1/3/96	2,313
30/12/94	1,913	4/8/95	2,153	8/3/96	2,268
6/1/95	1,868	11/8/95	2,128	15/3/96	2,235
13/1/95	1,859	18/8/95	2,102	22/3/96	2,245
20/1/95	1,878	25/8/95	2,117	29/3/96	2,226 Do
27/1/95	1,863	1/9/95	2,133	5/4/96	2,223
3/2/95	1,848	8/9/95	2,139	12/4/96	2,247
10/2/95	1,846	15/9/95	2,166	19/4/96	2,266
17/2/95	1,856	22/9/95	2,139	26/4/96	2,326 Up
24/2/95	1,911 Up	29/9/95	2,136	3/5/96	2,323
3/3/95	1,902	6/10/95	2,098	10/5/96	2,257
10/3/95	1,869	13/10/95	2,099	17/5/96	2,252
17/3/95	1,921	20/10/95	2,107	24/5/96	2,254
24/3/95	1,897	27/10/95	2,067 Do	31/5/96	2,266
31/3/95	1,907	3/11/95	2,092	7/6/96	2,220 Do

Date	Price	Date	Price	Date	Price
14/6/96	2,216	24/1/97	2,423	5/9/97	2,626
21/6/96	2,256	31/1/97	2,424	12/9/97	2,640
28/6/96	2,242	7/2/97	2,447	19/9/97	2,730 Up
5/7/96	2,231	14/2/97	2,483	26/9/97	2,776
12/7/96	2,160	21/2/97	2,475	3/10/97	2,763
19/7/96	2,158	28/2/97	2,450	10/10/97	2,695
26/7/96	2,143	7/3/97	2,439	17/10/97	2,646 Do
2/8/96	2,209	14/3/97	2,423	24/10/97	2,561
9/8/96	2,222 Up	21/3/97	2,386 Do	31/10/97	2,465
16/8/96	2,233	28/3/97	2,422	7/11/97	2,513
23/8/96	2,293	4/4/97	2,370	14/11/97	2,479
30/8/96	2,269	11/4/97	2,381	21/11/97	2,483
6/9/96	2,237	18/4/97	2,442	28/11/97	2,465
13/9/96	2,252	25/4/97	2,475 Up	5/12/97	2,557 Up
20/9/96	2,241	2/5/97	2,492	12/12/97	2,494
27/9/96	2,283	9/5/97	2,526	19/12/97	2,528
4/10/96	2,316	16/5/97	2,538	26/12/97	2,555
11/10/96	2,337	23/5/97	2,564	2/1/98	2,609
18/10/96	2,355	30/5/97	2,611	9/1/98	2,603
25/10/96	2,335	6/6/97	2,601	16/1/98	2,614
1/11/96	2,339	13/6/97	2,655	23/1/98	2,623
8/11/96	2,362	20/6/97	2,713	30/1/98	2,657
15/11/96	2,387	27/6/97	2,702	6/2/98	2,656
22/11/96	2,383	4/7/97	2,733	13/2/98	2,653
29/11/96	2,389	11/7/97	2,699	20/2/98	2,645
6/12/96	2,314	18/7/97	2,684	27/2/98	2,697
13/12/96	2,317	25/7/97	2,691	6/3/98	2,668
20/12/96	2,374	1/8/97	2,728	13/3/98	2,732
27/12/96	2,396	8/8/97	2,711	20/3/98	2,775
3/1/97	2,400	15/8/97	2,666	27/3/98	2,763
10/1/97	2,419	22/8/97	2,620 Do		
17/1/97	2,436	29/8/97	2,593		

Appendix D

CALCULATING THE A/D LINE USING EZY CHART PACKAGE

THE EZY CHART PACKAGE comprises the modules Ezy Chart, Ezy Analyser, Ezy Tools and Ezy Portfolio. There are a number of steps involved in building up an A/D line for an index spanning a number of years.

The major steps involved are:

1. Select an industry group.

2. Calculate the market statistics.

3. Build up the A/D file.

4. Display the A/D file as a chart.

BUILDING THE DAILY AOI A/D LINE

The steps in building the A/D line on the daily AOI are demonstrated below. The AOI has the Ezy Chart code xao.pce, and the daily A/D line data will be put into the user-defined file xaodad.pce. An intermediate stop involves generating the user-defined file aoist.ana, which holds the names of the stocks selected for A/D analysis.

Operations are for Ezy Chart Version 2.60 PLUS and Ezy Analyser Version 2.50. In the following discussion, text which appears on the screen are written in *italics*.

The reader may be discouraged by the number of key-strokes involved, but the initial effort is worthwhile as it becomes a simple matter to subsequently update the A/D data each day or week, say, and keep it up-to-date.

1. Select the Industry Group

Double click the icon on the desktop to open *Ezy Analyser*.
Click *1) Select Stocks*.
Click *Preselect*.

Make sure the lower screen radio buttons are set to *Industry Group* and *Select Individual Groups*.

We need to select the stocks from all the groups in the market. Thus, hold down key *Ctrl* and click all the *ASX Industry Groups* with the exception of the first group called *Unknown*. (This group holds overseas indices, local warrants etc.)

From the *Select All Codes* drop down window, click *Select Parent Codes*. (This selection ignores any preference shares, company options, etc. that may also be trading on a particular stock.)

Make sure the upper screen *Period* radio button is set to *Daily Data*.
Click *< < Preselect by Group*.
If nothing happens, click this box again. The upper left-hand side of the screen now scrolls through all the stocks in the ASX database and copies each of the parent codes (excluding those in the Unknown group) to the right-hand side display.
We must save this selection to the user-defined file *aoist.ana* for later use.

Click *Files* and from the drop down window click *Save Selection* then key in the *File name aoist.ana* making sure to remove the * from the file name.
Click *OK*.
Click *All Done*.

The screen now displays the Ezy Analyser desktop, but the top bar shows *Stocks Selected 984* which means that 984 stocks are selected from the full ASX list of stock codes.

2. Calculate Market Statistics

To calculate the market statistics, which in our case is the daily AOI A/D values, firstly open the Ezy Analyser and select the list of AOI stocks.

Click *Files* and from the drop down window click *Open Previous Selection* then key in the *File name aoist.ana*
Click *OK*.

The upper left-hand side of the screen displays the list of AOI parent stocks, and we move these to the active right-hand side of the screen.

Click *< < Select All*.
Click *> > Add > >*
Click *All Done*.

Once again the screen displays the Ezy Analyser desktop, and the top bar shows *Stocks Selected 984* which means that the 984 AOI stocks held in the *aoist.ana* list are selected.

3. Build up the A/D Line File

Now click the *Market Statistics* icon and enter the *Starting Date* and *Ending Date* values. The *Ending Date* is automatically set to today's date, while the *Starting Date* must be set no more than three years previously.
Click *Analyse Market* icon.
Click *Save Advance Decline Data* icon.
Key in the *File name aoidad.pce* making sure to remove the * from the file name.
Click *OK*.
The screen displays:

> *C:\EC\DATA\AOIDAD.PCE FOR ...*
> *Overwrite from this date forward?*

Select *Yes*.
Finally, click *RETURN* to return to the desktop menu.

4. Display the A/D File as a Chart

Double click the icon on the desktop to open Ezy Charts. Click *File* and from the drop down menu click *Open File*. Scroll down the file names and select *aoidad.pce*
Select the radio button *Daily Data*.
Click *Open*.
The daily A/D line chart is displayed on the screen.

5. Keeping the A/D Line Up-to-Date

Once the daily AOI A/D file is created, it can be kept up-to-date say each week by performing the previously described operations:

> Calculate Market Statistics
> Build Up the A/D File

When doing the Build Up the A/D File operation, the *Ending Date* is the current date, and the *Starting Date* is set to 5 days earlier. When we try to save the new file *aoidad.pce* the screen prompts:

> *Data exists in file C:\EC\DATA\AIODAD.PCE for ...*
> *Overwrite from this date forward?*

Click *Yes*.
Click *RETURN*.
The A/D line file *aoidad.pce* is now updated.

6. Aligning the AOI and A/D Line Plots

From time to time the daily AOI and A/D line plots need be printed to analyse for trend lines, divergences, etc. It is best to align both plots (as was done in Figure 14.1(a) and 14.1(b)).

To display the A/D line as a chart, double click the icon on the desktop to open Ezy Charts.
Click *File* and from the drop down menu click *Open File*.
Scroll down the file names and select *aoidad.pce*
The bottom part of the screen displays the *First Date* and *Last Date* for the A/D line.
Select the *Daily Data* radio button from the central section.

Under *Records to Load* there is a horizontal slider. Experiment with moving it fully left and fully right, and notice the varying number of *Daily Records*. Select a slider position resulting in, say, *500 Daily Records*.
Click *Open*.
A chart is drawn of the daily A/D line data spanning 500 days. This chart can be printed by clicking *File* followed by *Print Screen*.

The procedure is repeated with file *xao.pce*. It may be necessary to experiment with the position of the horizontal slider, to draw the daily AOI spanning exactly the same time frame as for the A/D line.

GLOSSARY

WHERE TERMS BELOW are applicable to options, equity warrants or index warrants, they will be defined for equity warrants.

Advance/Decline line Cumulative sum of daily stock rises and falls in a sector of the market.

ADX Average Directional Movement indicator which shows the strength of a stock's trend.

AII All Industrials Index.

Algorithm Set of mathematical calculations for a specific purpose.

AOAI All Ordinaries Accumulation Index, which gives the total return on share investment by including the value of dividends.

AOI All Ordinaries Index.

AOM Australian Options Market where options are traded.

At-market Order given to a broker to execute a transaction at the going market price.

At-the-money warrant Warrant whose exercise price is the same as the underlying share price.

ASX Australian Stock Exchange.

ATAA Australian Technical Analysts Association.

Back-test Feed historic stock data through a technical indicator to determine the indicator's performance over an earlier time period.

Blue chip stock Major stocks which are actively traded.

Breakout Stock price moves up or down out of a trading range or pattern.

BSOPM Black-Scholes Option Pricing Model.

Call warrant The right to buy a parcel of shares at a fixed price within a set time.

Coppock indicator Technical indicator developed by Edwin Coppock.

Defensive strategy Method of getting out of a losing trade with manageable loss.

Delta Ratio of warrant price move to stock price move.

Deposit Cash or securities held by a broker to cover the cost of trading options, warrants or short sales.

Derivative Financial product derived from something else, and having greater leverage than the "something else" from which it is derived.

DJIA Dow Jones Industrial Average.

DMI Directional movement indicator which shows a stock's sideways trends and breakouts.

Draw-down The amount the share price moves in the wrong direction after a trade is opened.

Equity warrant A one to two year put or call option on a stock, sponsored by a merchant bank or finance house.

ETOs Exchange traded options which are traded on the AOM.

Exercise of warrants Converting warrants to the underlying shares or to cash.

Exercise level Index level at which index warrants are converted.

Exercise price Stock price at which equity warrants are converted.

Expiry month Month that a warrant expires.

Exponential smoothing Method of smoothing data which gives more weight to the most recent data, and results in a faster response than SMA smoothing.

Filter Use of some form of second indicator to confirm the direction of a trade.

In-the-money warrant Call warrant whose exercise price is below the share price, or put warrant whose exercise price is above the share price.

Intrinsic value The share price minus the call warrant exercise price, or the put warrant exercise price minus the share price. Negative intrinsic value is set to 0.

Lagging indicator Indicator which gives a signal after the stock trend has changed.

Leading indicator Indicator which gives a signal or warning of an impending change in market trend.

Linear scale Chart vertical axis divided into equal numerical increments.

Logarithmic scale (or Semi-log scale) Chart vertical axis divided into equal percentage increments.

Long position Holding a position in anticipation of an upward move.

MACD Moving average convergence divergence technical indicator used to determine stock trends.

Margin call Cash to be paid to the broker to cover an open trade which moves in the wrong direction.

Momentum indicator Technical indicator that tells when a trend is either gathering strength, or running out of steam.

Money management Proportioning the size of a trade and the potential trading profits and losses to the size of trading kitty.

Noise Small variations in price which are secondary to the trend, but which sometimes trigger technical indicators erroneously.

NYSE New York Stock Exchange.

Option stocks Blue chip stocks on which exchange traded options are available.

Oscillators (momentum oscillators) Technical indicators which show when a stock is overbought/oversold and due for a change in trend.

Out-of-the-money warrant Call warrant whose strike price is above the share price, or put warrant whose strike price is below the share price.

Parcel size Minimum number of warrants that can be traded.

Percent Model Technical indicator based on a specific percentage reversal in a trend.

Pullback The amount the share price reverses after a fresh price move.

Put warrant The right to sell a parcel of shares at a fixed price within a set time.

Pyramiding Increasing the size of a trade after the initial investment shows a profit.

Rats and mice Small capitalisation stocks with dubious worth.

Risk-free interest rate Term deposit interest rate available from a bank or finance house.

Risk—return Balancing the possible risk (loss) against the possible return (profit) in a trade.

Semi-log scale – see *Logarithmic scale*

Short position Holding a position in anticipation of a downward move.

Short selling Selling shares not owned with the intent of buying them back later at a lower price.

Slippage Difference between theoretical price and actual price achieved in executing an order.

SMA indicator Single moving average indicator used to determine stock trends.

SPI Share Price Index, being a futures contract on the AOI.

Stops Predetermined exit points on a trade.

System equity Term used by SuperCharts software to describe the cumulative profit and loss over a number of trades.

Technical analysis Use of technical indicators and charts to determine past and future share price behaviour.

Technical indicator A set of mathematical calculations on share price or volume data, resulting in some form of graphical display, that gives information on the stock trends.

Technical stop Stop set just below a support line, or just above a resistance line.

Time to expiry Number of days, weeks or months to the expiry of a warrant.

Time premium Warrant price minus intrinsic value.

Trading range Where prices move sideways within a horizontal channel for some time.

Trading strategy Trading rules incorporating both trading system and money management procedures.

Trading system Selection of technical indicators and charting techniques used to determine the start and end of stock trends.

Trend-following indicator Indicator which gives a signal after the stock trend has changed.

Turning point Price (or time) at which one trade is closed, and a fresh one opened in the opposite direction.

Turtles Group of specially taught successful traders.

VLI Value Line Index.

Volatility Share price activity that is reflected in the warrant price.

Warrant A contract to either buy or sell a specific number of shares in a particular stock, at a given price, up to a given time.

Warrant stocks Blue chip stocks on which warrants are available.

Whipsaw Price hiccup which closes a trade, opens a new one in the opposite direction, then reverses again to close the new trade at a loss.

Wizards (market wizards) Champion traders popularised by Schwager's book *Market Wizards*.

Index

50% of trades profitable 20, 178

Account drawdown 179
Advance/decline line 77-83
—calculation of 81
—calculation using Ezy Chart Package 224-227
—for AII 116-117
—for AOI 79-80
—for All Resources Index 123-125
—for Gold Index 109-110
Advance/decline ratio 26, 82
All Industrials Index (AII) 11-12, 15, 66
—analysis of – *see* MACD, *etc.*
All Ordinaries Accumulation Index (AOAI) 10-11, 153
All Ordinaries Index (AOI) 8-10, 15, 21, 66
—analysis of – *see* MACD, *etc.*
—trading index warrants on 181
—weekly data for 219-223
All Resources Index 13, 15
—analysis of, *see* MACD, *etc.*
Allocation per trade 178, 179
AMP 158-159
Annual return 9, 10, 12, 14, 17, 26, 62, 153, 154, 156, 157, 159, 160, 162, 163, 171, 191
Appel, Gerald 33
Argo Investments 156, 188, 191
Armstrong, Merril 79
Australian Economics, Strategy & Equity Research 102
Australian Financial Review 81, 204
Australian Foundation Investment Company (AFIC) 154-156, 188, 191

The Australian Investor's Guide to Charting 101
Australian Stock Exchange (ASX) 9, 102, 103
Australian Technical Analysts Association (ATAA) 23, 83, 198, 199, 204
—journal 23, 25
Average Directional Movement Index (ADX) 43-46, 47

Back-testing 20-22, 93
Bankers Trust (BT) Listed Companies 159-162
—BT Australian Equities 159-160
—BT Global 161-162
—BT Resources 160-161
Barclays Investment Funds 166-167
BBL Investment Funds 167
Benchmark Australian All Ordinaries Index Trust (BAT) 164-165, 191
—trading 180
—trading using technical stops 181
Benchmark results on weekly AOI 34, 36
—3.5 Percent Model comparison 63
—weekly SMA comparison 51
—weekly Coppock comparison 74
Black-Scholes Option Pricing Model (BSOPM) 141
Bolton-Smith, Dawn 72, 79
Bonus issues 154, 156, 157
Box size 85-86, 88
Brokers 19
Buffet, Warren 153, 178

Chart patterns 101
Compound return – *see* Annual return